TRUE SOUTH

Leadership Lessons From Polar Extremes

J. PHILLIPS L. JOHNSTON, J.D.

Prospecta Press
Westport

TRUE SOUTH copyright © 2014 by J. Phillips L. Johnston

All rights reserved. No portion of this book may be reproduced in any fashion, print, facsimile, or electronic, or by any method yet to be developed, without the express written permission of the publisher.

Manufactured in the United States of America

First edition published May 2014 by Prospecta Press

www.prospectapress.com

Paperback ISBN 978-1-63226-002-4

eBook ISBN 978-1-63226-003-1

Photographs:
Portrait of Amundsen, Keystone-France/Getty Images

Man-Hauling by Brits, Captain Scott/Popperfoto/Getty Images

Amundsen and fellow Norwegians using sextant at the Pole, Universal Images Group/Getty Images

The Norwegian national monument commemorating the first men to reach the South Pole: Roald Amundsen, Helmer Hanssen, Oscar Wisting, Olav Bjaaland and Sverre Hassel by Cornelius Poppe, December 2011/AFP/Getty Images

Portrait of Scott in full uniform, Time Life Pictures/Getty Images

At the head of the table, Captain Scott Celebrates his 43rd and last birthday; Scott Polar Research, University of Cambridge/Popperfoto/Getty Images

Illustrations:
Map of the location of One Ton © J. Phillips L. Johnston 2014

Amundsen's Light/Heavy Leadership © J. Phillips L. Johnston 2014

Graphic illustrations by North Street Creative

Cover design by Barbara Aronica-Buck

Cover image courtesy Captain Scott/Popperfoto/Getty Images

The labor of this book is dedicated to Louise, Bea, and Edie Renwick and Charlotte Johnston, who have brought unbounded joy into my life. One day when you become young ladies, you can take this book from some upper shelf, dust it off, and tell me what you think of it. Let me know if you believe in the supreme importance and imperative of leadership in all endeavors for the betterment of mankind. I shall probably be too deaf to hear, and too old to understand a word you say, but I will still be your loving Grandpapa.

Amundsen and his fellow heroes, as immortalized at The Maritime Museum in Oslo, claimed the last frontier with ten hands planting the Norwegian flag as one.

CONTENTS

	Preface	vii
	Foreword	ix
	Author's Note	xiii
	Prologue	xiv
	Message to the Public	xvi
1.	Antarctica: Where Beauty Belies Death	1
2.	Scott and His Party Succumb to the Elements	5
3.	Leadership: The Ability to Unify and Influence Others Toward Positive Goals	10
4.	Amundsen: A Case Study in Unified Mission, Calculated Strategy, and Analytical Preparation	13
5.	Scott's Mission, Strategy, and Planning	25
6.	Polar-Opposite Leadership: Élan, Improvisation and Gutsiness Versus Blinding Speed	47
7.	Formation of Values Then and Now	52
8.	Amundsen's Early Years	56
9.	Scott's Early Years	63
10.	Values: Where the Buck Begins	69

11.	C H A L L E N G E S: Pointing True South Toward Leadership Excellence	72
12.	Morality	93
13.	A Closing Word on Followership	96
14.	Epilogue: Amundsen's Tarnished Gold in Retirement	103
	The Cast	109
	Timeline of Events in Amundsen's and Scott's Lifetimes	121
	Appendix: List of Firsts by Amundsen	129
	Cliff Notes on the History of Leadership	131
	Leadership Myths	135
	Why Would These Men Willingly Subject Themselves to such Unthinkable Hazards and Hardships as the Assault on the South Pole?	139
	Acknowledgements	141
	Selected Bibliography	145
	About the Author	147

PREFACE

True South is uncharted territory in the world of leadership: an in-depth comparison of leadership practices that succeed and fail, observed from the petri dish of the last terrestrial frontier. Ravaged by ripping winds and miles of unspeakable peril in their epic race to claim the South Pole, famed explorers Roald Amundsen and Robert Scott are pitted against each other and the cruel Antarctic terrain, risking their lives with every step. Swept into the century-old narrative, today's reader will discover the needed navigational tools for a lifetime of values-based entrepreneurial leadership along the way. With lessons harvested from these brave explorers' polar diaries, travelers to *True South* will discover that Amundsen was a full century ahead of his time in his:

- Elegant strategy
- Encouragement of heavy followership
- Embodiment of the ten most enduring traits for aspiring leaders in any field, outlined in the mnemonic, CHALLENGES
- Recognition of the value of diversity of thought

From the contemporaneous failures of Amundsen's polar opposite, Robert Scott, cautionary illustrations are charted for the would-be leader, detailing the dangers of:

- Groupthink

- Lack of strategy and contingency planning
- People selection based on petty favoritism
- Authoritarian self-entitlement

The leadership lessons from the polar extremes of Antarctica map the way forward in a world that often seems to have lost its bearings.

FOREWORD

In his dialogue *Phaedo*, Plato famously asks whether virtue can be *taught*. In simplest terms, he answers that, while it cannot be taught, it can be learned; and we might argue the same about a subject that has absorbed the attention of business – and government, students of organizational behavior, the military establishment, and universities – for a generation: *leadership*. Contemporary academia, seduced by the national interest in leadership, invariably advertises "programs" in leadership, builds "centers" for its study, and hires corporate leaders to deliver commencement addresses. All this activity is harmless, and, so far as the identification and transmission of expertise and technique are concerned, even useful.

Two distinct American generations, each prodigal in the production of leaders – political, civic, military – had little idea of academic training for "leadership." The first of these, once a staple of scrutiny by Americans in their high school years, comprised the Founders – the Adamses, Jefferson, Washington, Hamilton – men educated in the histories of Greece and, particularly, Rome, and in the lives of their leaders, lives inflected by testing crises and the severest of challenges. When we ask ourselves where such figures "came from," we enter at once into the amorphous realm of human *character*. The complex of human qualities subsumed under that word cannot be taught with any confidence that such instruction will influence, for good, the young people who are its objects.

The generation of American military leaders that saw the nation successfully through the Second World War was thick with sons of the American outback: youngsters raised in hardscrabble circumstances in which qualities of self-reliance, diligence, and selflessness were deeply laid. Such things, it was believed, could not be *taught* but must be acquired only through living.

But, as Phil Johnston's *True South* powerfully and persuasively argues, such elements of character are not enough. In the memorable competition of the opening years of the 20th Century between the Englishman Captain Robert Scott and the Norwegian Roald Amundsen to be the first to claim arrival at the South Pole, a contest that achieved worldwide celebrity, memorable lessons in leadership are present. Chief among these is that the veriest of late Victorian virtues – pluck – is, however noble, not enough. Hardihood and stoic allegiance to mission, whatever the costs, however admirable, are rarely alone sources of success. Captain Scott, whose noble death along with those of his four companions inspired and evoked unstinted admiration from a nation anxious for heroes, was enshrined in the British pantheon of heroic conduct. (King George V attended memorial services in St. Paul's Cathedral.) But Scott had failed as a leader out of purblind ignorance of enduring principles of leading other persons in a simple – if challenging – mission.

Johnston contrasts the circumstances of Scott's upbringing and education as a scion of an upper-class English family and as a midshipman in the Royal Navy in which "unquestioning obedience to authority… became his marching code, to the detriment of his ability to think independently." In his 1912 trek across the pitiless landscape of the South Pole, Scott ignored his men's suggestions, criticisms, and ideas, while managing throughout his diaries to place blame for the expedition's misfortunes "squarely on bad luck with the weather." Eventually, in Johnston's words, "the ice silently swallowed him up, along with his team…as they began to perish staggering from exhaustion, snowblindness, scurvy, gangrene, dehydration, and hypothermia." Their remains were found months after their deaths in March of 1912. Scott's rival Amundsen, on the contrary, bespeaks a character whose principal element would appear to be humility – humility uniquely combined with an unassuageable thirst to learn more from those he led and a willingness to mistrust received wisdom. He was a man of compassion, a team player, what a later generation calls a "servant leader," always willing to employ new techniques to accomplish his mission. Scott endorsed what to a later age seems an insane attachment to human haulage, members of his team hauling their possessions and provisions (and equipment for scientific measurement) on foot; Amundsen's team used dogs and sleds and traversed the 1700 miles roundtrip on skis.

The virtue and utility of *True South* inheres in the memorable legacies of human conduct in circumstances of unimaginable stress and danger – conduct directly the consequence of the nature of leadership provided. This small book seems to me inestimably more valuable as a source of leadership lessons than virtually all analyses and reflections on the subject to eager generations of students enrolled in "leadership centers."

Josiah Bunting III
HF Guggenheim Foundation

Mr. Bunting is chairman of the English Speaking Union (US) and president of the HF Guggenheim Foundation in New York City. After graduating from VMI, he attended Oxford University as a Rhodes Scholar and Columbia University, where he was a John Burgess Fellow. As a major in the US Army, he taught history at West Point and the Naval War College, later serving as president or head of several educational institutions, including The Lawrenceville School, VMI, Briarcliff College, Hampden Sydney College, and ISI's Lehrman American Studies Center, an annual two-week colloquium at Princeton for PhDs who teach government, political science, American history, or economics. Among his publications are several novels, including *The Lionheads*, selected as one of the Ten Best Novels of 1973 by *Time* magazine, and *An Education for Our Time,* a utopian fantasy about an ideal college; a biography of *Ulysses S. Grant* (Times Books/Henry Holt, part of the *American Presidents* series, edited by Arthur M. Schlesinger Jr.); and a new venture to be published by Knopf on the life of George C. Marshall.

AUTHOR'S NOTE

Despite thousands of attempts to produce a definitive primer on the highly complex subject of leadership, no such book has emerged over two millennia dating back to Plato. Maybe after the twenty-four-hundred-year wait, it is time to admit that an authoritative Leadership How-To is not a realistic, or even a desirable goal. Leadership is not a subject to be fully mastered; it is a never-ending pilgrimage, one that is often fraught with pitfalls and detours, but nonetheless is loaded with treasure at every turn. The hope herein is that the story of Roald Amundsen and Robert Scott's race to claim the last frontier on earth, told from the vantage point of their leadership successes and failures, will prove a valuable reference on your journey.

Enjoy the venture as you navigate the way leading to True South.

PROLOGUE

The British public's outpouring of grief in February of 1913 for the five fallen heroes lost in the epic battle to claim the South Pole was profound, exceeding even the widespread desolation following the sinking of the *Titanic* on April 15, 1912. According to the prestigious British daily newspaper the *Manchester Guardian*, "Nothing in our time, scarcely even the foundering of the *Titanic* has touched the whole nation so instantly and so deeply as the loss of these men."

Captain Robert Scott's now-famous "Message to the Public" was read to an estimated million and a half schoolchildren from Cardiff to Carlisle and was published in every newspaper in England. The "Message," written in back of Scott's final notebook, claimed the disaster was "not due to faulty organization, but to misfortune in all risks which had to be undertaken." The solemnity and initial impact of Scott's message to the British public rivaled the grave delivery of the Gettysburg Address. Both were considered stunning masterpieces in their appeal for the preservation of a national identity, each giving breadth and depth to heroic deaths of fellow countrymen. Appealing to God Almighty and a higher calling at a historically significant moment, both messages were written for the unification and mended spirit of a faltering nation.

Further heightening the dramatic impact of the British tragedy, King George V himself attended the memorial service honoring the five polar explorers at St. Paul's Cathedral on February 14, 1913. Regally clad in the uniform of Admiral of the Fleet and flanked by military and government dignitaries, the monarch presided in an ornate armchair under the expansive dome facing the magnificent altar, as "The Dead March" from Handel's *Saul* moved mourners to tears. In an era when the throne was all-powerful, it was highly unusual for the reigning monarch to personally attend a funeral or memorial service of non-royalty. The king, like the thousands standing in the dank shroud of gloom outside the cathedral, wanted to have a personal connection with the honored dead.

MESSAGE TO THE PUBLIC

We are weak, writing is difficult, but, for my own sake, I do not regret this journey, which has shown that Englishmen can endure hardship, help one another and meet death with as great a fortitude as ever in the past.

We took risks—we knew we took them.

Things have come out against us, and therefore we have no cause for complaint, but bow to the will of providence, determined still to do our best till the last.

But if we have been willing to give our lives to this enterprise, which is for the honour of our country, I appeal to our countrymen to see that those who depend on us are properly provided for.

Had we lived I should have had a tale to tell of the hardihood, endurance, and courage of my companions which would have stirred the heart of every Englishman.

These rough notes and our dead bodies must tell the tale; but surely, surely, a great rich country like ours will see that those who are dependent on us are properly provided for.

Why did Scott's "Message to the Public" resonate so forcefully in Edwardian Britain and give birth to a heroic legend?

First, Scott was already revered as a widely acclaimed explorer and author of *The Voyage of the Discovery*, which detailed his first expedition to Antarctica from 1901–1904 and received rave reviews. Even though it is the only full-length book Scott ever published, it is magnificently written and catapulted Scott high atop the crow's nest of popular acclaim, effectively establishing him as the unchallenged authority on polar exploration. Scott's rhetorical skills and considerable gifts as a writer equipped him to gloss over the numerous shortcomings of the expedition and conceal his leadership flaws. Today Scott's legacy is not as the great explorer of a bygone era; instead he is remembered because he composed the most haunting journal in the history of exploration.

Scott's "Message" served as a powerful testament giving voice to the heroic fantasies of his generation as the sun was setting on the British Empire, when its position was being supplanted by the United States as world superpower during World War I. Evidence that Britain was highly protective and proud of their lofty, dominant position seeps out in the polar journals revealing a society focused on national pride built on the entitlement of inbred class and social rank rather than on merit and work ethic. This was a time that British "pluck" and "stiff upper lip" continued to be greatly admired, frequently voiced, but in truth, rarely practiced.

Still, Scott's "Message to the Public" was received and interpreted as a triumphant retort to the prophets of decline, just as he fully intended it. The British monthly *Wide World Magazine* proclaimed that Scott's message was "the most impressive document ever read by man." Indeed, the outpouring of public donations was $7.2 million in today's dollars, enough to pay off all the expedition's debts, publish the scientific results, erect a memorial, and provide more than adequately for the bereaved.

Scott's persona added greatly to the high drama and grandeur of the tragedy, regarded as he was as upper-class nobility, a consummate gentlemen for all seasons and an insightful writer who understood his audience's romantic view of duty, struggle, and sacrifice. His heroic narrative was undergirded by his reputation as a scholar, an absolutely faithful husband, and selfless provider who supported his mother and siblings when his father's brewery went bankrupt in 1894. Sampson-like in strength and brave beyond belief in the face of death, he who had commanded several battleships where all seven hundred or more men aboard revered the captain as if he were a god still commanded the respect of an admiring nation.

Feeding the frenzy of his burgeoning popularity was the simple fact that the man had an overabundance of that beloved British quality—pluck: what a chap can do if he is made of the right stuff.

Over the last fifty years, however, Scott's leadership deficiencies have gradually diminished the glow of his many sterling qualities. Scott's wife, with even more formidable influence as Lady Kennet in her next marriage, defended the legend of Scott's duty, struggle, and sacrifice, sensationalizing his death with her sticky tenacity until she died in 1947. Regrettably, it has been discovered that she was guilty of doctoring her dead husband's journals by lowering temperatures and deleting certain unflattering entries. In 1977, David Thompson, author of *Scott's Men*, was one of the first historians to suggest that Scott was not necessarily such a great man, "at least, not until near the end." He describes the famed explorer's planning as "haphazard" and "flawed." Thompson further notes Scott's "complex personality" and repeatedly questions Scott's methods.

In 1979 historian Roland Huntford eviscerates Scott in his published account of the race to the South Pole, *Scott and Amundsen*. According to Huntford, "He personified the glorious failure which by now had become a British ideal. He was a suitable hero of a nation in decline."

Huntford adds a final blow to the solar plexus, if not lower: "Scott was a heroic bungler. He added nothing to the technique of Polar travel, unless it was to emphasize the grotesque futility of man-hauling."

A new orthodoxy had emerged concerning Scott's legacy, in part because the Great World Wars were over, as was the hero-worshiping of the time. It was almost as if historians banded together to form a Board of Inquiry about the Scott's role in the Race. In 2002, Scott's ranking in the "British 100" listing plunged to fifty-fourth, while Ernest Shackleton's zoomed to eleventh place. Today the market value of the original "Message to the

Public" has swooned to a mere $250,000, while the five known copies of the "Gettysburg Address" in Lincoln's hand are valued at seventeen to twenty-two million dollars each.

Concurrently, awakening from the ashes of a hundred year sleep, Amundsen's legacy has been exhumed and dusted off during this collective "second look"—a recasting for which Scott provided the fulcrum. An additional boost has occurred with the recent translation of most of Amundsen's and his fellow Norwegians' journals, letters, and speeches. Even though Amundsen was greatly hindered by his lack of flare in speaking and writing about his adventures, he has always been considered a giant of an explorer. It is now clear from the corroboration of all journals and letters that his leadership and strategic skills account for his stature as the towering figure in the history of exploration.

This is the likely to be the first of many books that will hoist Amundsen, with his perfection of heavy followership, into the pantheon of great leaders. Unlike the revisionist historians of the last fifty years, you will certainly find Scott's gentlemanly sense of honor to be worthy of study and emulation in the intercourse of a meaningful life and establishing an appropriate value system for leadership. However, amid his ascent to the top, Scott's quest for leadership greatness collided with the hubris endemic in Edwardian England, further compounded by the attending groupthink of that same rigid class system. Nonetheless, in terms of his code of ethics, fidelity, and balanced intellect, Scott provides sturdy scaffolding from which to apply the ten leadership traits perfected by Amundsen. The two polar opposites in leadership are, amazingly, opposites in both their strengths and weaknesses; that is to say, Scott's sterling qualities as a scholar and a gentleman are proportional to Amundsen's deficits in that regard, just as Amundsen's acumen as a leader and strategist represent a similarly dark void in Scott's overall picture.

If Mary Shelly could overlay the patterns of these two fascinating explorers, a Lincoln, a Churchill, or a Mahatma Gandhi likeness would be created in Ingolstadt.

But let's be clear: Scott was not a heroic bungler. He had chronic leadership flaws that proved deadly as he became an arrogant and willing participant in the tragic groupthink orchestrated by Clements Markham, but a bungler he was not.

CHAPTER 1.

ANTARCTICA: WHERE BEAUTY BELIES DEATH

Antarctica, the continent surrounding the South Pole, is twice the size of Europe. Perhaps part of its allure is the mystery and emptiness of this killer continent. This kaleidoscope of ice has earned the reputation as the most extreme environment on earth, an inhospitable place where killer whales, seals, and penguins survive—but little else.

Most of her land lies buried beneath the masses of ice and snow two miles deep in East Antarctica covering the Gamburtsev Subglacial Mountains, a range more massive than the Alps. She holds the record for the coldest weather ever registered: minus 126.9 degrees Fahrenheit in August 1960 at Vostok Station, the location of Lake Vostok, the largest of more than four hundred subglacial lakes below the Antarctic ice sheet. After two decades of drilling, Russian researchers recently made contact with the gigantic freshwater lake at a depth of 12,366 feet. Lake Vostok could hold living organisms that have been locked in icy darkness for some twenty million years, as well as clues in the search for life elsewhere in the solar system.[1]

The relentless freezing wind gusting up to two hundred miles per hour rages across the frozen surface dusted with snow raking her ragged surface. Antarctica's deafening eeriness is compounded by the incessant moans and haunting shrieks as the ice creates its own devilment caused by the constant motion of its glaciers. All the while, ensconced within her hardened grip is more fresh water than the entire rest of our planet.[2]

Though desolate, her beauty is unmatched. In the thin, dry atmosphere of Antarctica, the clarity of light is a stargazer's dream and the inspiration for China's large new Plateau Observatory. Without any man-made distractions in her evening sky, one feels emboldened to reach up and pluck a star out of the magnificent canopy stretched into eternity. Not to be outdone by the northern lights, her southern counterpart, aurora australis, paints an exquisite portrait on her Southern Hemisphere canvas. As protons and electrons shot from the sun strike the upper atmosphere, the earth's magnetic field accelerates the particles toward her magnetic pole, forming long curtains of flickering frost-white, green, and red beams.

The slightly saline, pristine waters surrounding Antarctica glisten with dazzling beauty. Mountains protrude through the ice cap in the interior and outline much of her coast. Majestic rivers of ice grind slowly down to the sea from valleys perched high among the soaring Transantarctic Mountains, rising as high at sixteen thousand feet. The glaciers, especially Beardmore and Axel Heiberg, swell the heart in their panoramic wonder, even while dispensing terrifying avalanches at their rims.

As glaciers constantly creep to the sea, sharp crevasses are formed as deep as a mile below the ice surface with widths as narrow as an inconspicuous sliver to as wide as a boat deck. Wind whipping across the expanse of open ice carves out wave-like ridges called sastrugi, all with the deft strokes of a Picasso. This visual symphony of stark white is largely unaffected by snowfall; the pole itself receives only four to six inches annually.

Another breathtaking spectacle is the calving of massive sections of the glaciers some 250 feet in height into the Ross Sea, frequently preceded by what sounds like a triple thunderclap. Glacier calving is a form of ice ablation usually following the exact lines of the open crevasse formations. The implosion of the massive chunks of the glacier cascading into the Ross Sea marks the birth of an iceberg. The resulting wake can capsize boats as far as two miles away. Arguably, nothing in nature is more awe-inspiring than glacier calving.

The beauty of the ice captivates. She is a relentless seductress, wooing adventurers with all her charm into her irresistible chambers; then at the moment of submission, the ice takes the life of her prey and snuffs it out with the icy coolness of a Latrodectus. One can never let down his guard with this Narnian queen as she reigns over her unforgiving expanse of white in all its drop-dead allure; one must outwit, outthink, and out-strategize her at every turn.

So now we turn to the diaries of the two revered Antarctic explorers whose accounts ever bear witness to their wit, strategy, and leadership styles: Two polar-opposite leaders pitted against each other as they are lured by the siren call of the ice.

Notes

1. The temperature of the lake is about −22.6°F, but the water remains liquid because of the pressure exerted by the ice sheet. The pressure also keeps the water super-saturated with oxygen and nitrogen. Most of the creatures discovered will be tiny single-celled microbes, visible only under a microscope, but they will have novel genetic structures. The organisms will use previously undiscovered enzymes and will have evolved unique survival strategies. According to Bryan Appleyard's article, "Some Like it Very Hot" in <i>Intelligent Life </i>Magazine May/June 2012, these creatures, known as extremophiles, or lovers of extreme conditions, will likely offer a cornucopia of new medical compounds, primarily antibiotics, as well as almost indestructible enzymes that could transform chemistry both domestically and industrially.

2. The Antarctic continent contains more than 80 percent of the world's fresh water. Thousands of icebergs are naturally released each year. French marine engineer Georges Mougin has long dreamed of towing

Antarctica's ice mountains through the water across the globe, realizing their enormous potential of delivering fresh water to desert cities throughout the world.

CHAPTER 2.

SCOTT AND HIS PARTY SUCCUMB TO THE ELEMENTS

Curiosity concerning morbidity is timeless and universal; lean in as Robert Falcon Scott, suffering from scurvy and badly frostbitten gangrenous feet, somberly pens his final diary entry on March 29, 1912:

> Since the 21st we have had a continuous gale from wsw and sw. We had fuel to make two cups of tea apiece and bare food for two days on the 20th. Every day we have been ready to start for our depot 11 miles away, but outside the door of the tent it remains a scene of whirling drift. I do not think we can hope for better things now. We shall stick it out to the end, but we are getting weaker of course, and the end cannot be far. It seems a pity, but I do not think I can write more. R. Scott.

Food and fuel awaited them at One Ton Depot eleven miles away! Hut Point on the banks of McMurdo Sound was less than one hundred miles from One Ton.

During the three months prior to his last entry on that fateful March day, Scott and his men had successfully man-hauled sledges ninety-five hundred feet up the Beardmore Glacier, and then across the Polar Plateau. On January 16, 1912, Bower's sharp eyes spotted a black dot in the distance. Moving closer, everyone's heart sank as a flapping marker flag materialized giving form to the dot, and they began to see that the snow was etched with ski tracks dotted with dog prints before the Norwegian flag and tent confirmed the dreaded truth. Scott expressed their shared anguish that day in his famous diary entry:

> This told us the whole story. The Norwegians have forestalled us and are first at the Pole. It is a terrible disappointment, and I am very sorry for my loyal companions. Many thoughts come and much discussion we have had. Tomorrow we must march on the Pole, and then hasten home with all the speed we can compass. All the day-dreams must go; it will be a wearisome return.

The next day Scott reached the South Pole facing rabid headwinds and temperatures of minus 22 degrees Fahrenheit, giving three men frostbite. On January 17 came his heart-wrenching climactic diary entry:

> A horrible day...
> Great God! This is an awful place and terrible enough for us to have laboured to it without the reward of priority.

The journals reveal that five British polar explorers on the return trip down the Beardmore Glacier and the Ross Ice Shelf died at the hand of Captain Robert Falcon Scott. Their deaths were a direct result of his leadership failure exacerbated by the groupthink of the British polar leadership hierarchy. Several diaries of the other twelve British explorers who left Cape Evans in detachments on November 1, 1911 for the 1,766 miles to the pole and back corroborate this abject failure of leadership.[1]

On the other hand, Roald Amundsen personifies leadership acumen, and his light is placed on a lamp stand as an example to all who aspire to be leaders. He was the first man to stand on the geographic South Pole just over one hundred years ago on December 14, 1911. This death-defying feat of heroism was achieved thirty-five days before the arrival of Scott's group. Five Norwegian men with their sixteen dog companions planted the Norwegian flag *together*. On top of the world at the bottom of the world, Amundsen insisted that each man's hand grasp the flagpole as they staked their claim; he recorded the day's events:

"So at that we reached our destination and planted our flag on the geographical South Pole, King Haakon VII's Plateau. Thank God!"

After renaming the Antarctic Plateau in honor of the Norwegian king, he named the area of their little tent *Polheim*, or "Home on the Pole." They left a letter there stating their accomplishment in case they did not return safely to Framheim at the Bay of Whales.[2] The Norwegian team in fact returned, reaching their home base on January 25, 1912, with eleven dogs and all five men in excellent health. Amundsen's heroism was publicly announced on March 7, 1912, when he arrived at Hobart, Australia.

Laying their diaries side by side, along with the many accounts by their fellow polar explorers, Amundsen's leadership style stands in polar opposite to Scott's. In contrast to their Norwegian counterparts, all five British explorers died agonizing deaths at the hands of the monster ice. Her siren call had cast its spell, and indeed, the Antarctic continent had beckoned her guests to come and die there. The tent entombing the frozen bodies of Lieutenant Henry Bowers, Dr. Edward Wilson, and Captain Robert Scott was not discovered until November 12, 1912, almost eight months after their deaths. The tent was collapsed over the three bodies forming an oversized ossuary. Nearby, the search party erected a great cairn of ice surmounted by a cross made from skis and planted a sledge nose-first in a smaller cairn close by.

A search was mounted for brave Captain Oates's body, but it was never found, only his discarded sleeping bag, cut open for much of the length to enable Oates to enter it with his badly frostbitten, gangrenous feet. Another cairn was placed at the search area to commemorate Oates's heroism and etched with the words that beckon his legendary chivalry: "Hereabouts died a very gallant gentleman."

On their return to Hut Point at McMurdo Sound, a cross made of jarrah wood bearing the final line of Tennyson's "Ulysses"—"To strive, to seek, to find, and not to yield"—was erected on

Observation Hill on January 20, 1913, in memory of:

> Lieutenant H. R. Bowers
> Petty Officer Edgar Evans
> Captain L. E. G. Oates
> Captain R. F. Scott
> Dr. E. A. Wilson

Even though Oates's and Evans's bodies were separated in death from the other three and never found, all five will be rejoined in the year 2275 as their remains, entombed in the glaciers, slowly inch toward the sea at a rate gradually accelerating to over three thousand feet a year, and then finally calve into their permanent icy grave in the Ross Sea for eternity.

Alas, when the merciless Barrier releases its grip on Scott, Wilson and Bowers, followed by Oates and then Evans, these restless explorers will be reunited in their final watery resting place not segregated by a lower deck. In death, leaders join followers; as God clears life's chessboard, the king and the pawn reside in the same box. While born equal in the eyes of God, all are not valued equally in the competition of life and living. Death is the great equalizer as we return to the breast of our Creator.

Notes

1. "From Hut Point to the South Pole and back is 1,532 geographical or 1,766 statute miles," according to The Worst Journey in the World, by Aspley Cherry-Garrard (Chapter IX, p. 189 of the Empire Books edition published in 2011). Wikipedia confirms that the round-trip distance from Cape Evans to the South Pole is 1,766 miles and from the Bay of Whales is 1,700 miles. There are discrepancies throughout the literature: Bjaaland's diary says "1,400 miles" round-trip, while Huntford states "1,500" in the opening chapter of *The Last Place on*

Earth. He further says on p. 378, "144 days for the 1,530 miles to the pole and back, a saving of 120 miles in a journey of 1,364 miles as the crow files, or almost 9%." Although not stated, both Bjaaland and Huntford are using geographic miles (taking into account the curvature of the earth), not statute miles (1,760 yards; 5, 280 feet). To top off the debate, most resources state that Shackleton traveled "1,730 miles" before turning back at 88°, 23'. Being exactly 97 miles from the pole, 1, 824 would be the round-trip distance in miles. Hut Point, base camp during the Discovery Expedition, is 12 miles closer to the pole than Cape Evans (also known as Scott's Hut). Even on the Terra Nova Expedition, Scott used Hut Point as a second base camp. Some references to distances confuse the two. Even though both parties depended on the accuracy of sledge meters, the correct distances used today are 1,700 from the Bay of Whales and 1,766 miles from Hut Point.

2. Raymond Priestley, one of the British geologists on the expedition, later observed that at that moment Scott "was degraded from explorer to postman" by Amundsen. Amundsen, of course, was merely taking precautions against the chance that he might perish on his return.

CHAPTER 3.

LEADERSHIP: THE ABILITY TO UNIFY AND INFLUENCE OTHERS TOWARD POSITIVE GOALS

The principles of leadership are, in the main, mushy, elusive, and very subjective. Strong leadership by the board of directors, the ultimate depository of corporate power, and the chief executive officer is essential to the very survival of free market capitalism. With boards at the pinnacle of power, some have suggested that succession planning, enterprise risk management, and strategy make up the governance centerpiece.

In British jurisprudence, a modern estimation of the key to board greatness adds an important dimension: "entrepreneurial leadership"—which widens the definition to include innovative and pattern solutions found at the edge of and beyond traditional methods. Entrepreneurship is best thought of as uncommon solutions to common challenges, without the constraints of budgets, at least initially. The more risk, the more substantial is the reward.

Observing lessons from the race to the South Pole, the term further expands to "compassionate entrepreneurial leadership." This new definition personified by Roald Amundsen adds the important dimension of values. It is this term that moves companies up the rung from good to great. Compassionate entrepreneurial leadership applies at both the board level and throughout the C-suite: Compass needle True South is the leadership metaphor and Amundsen's trademark.

Without compassionate entrepreneurial leadership, the United States of America will never, ever restore its position as a world leader. Double-digit unemployment is less about Joseph Schumpeter's creative destruction of the industrial revolution and more about policemen, construction workers, and firemen garnering *substantially* more respect and trust than the leaders of capitalism. Managers and directors now rank only slightly higher than politicians in opinion polls, a more stinging slap to the face than a blast of Antarctic wind.[1] The restoration of values-based entrepreneurial leadership is critical to our children's future: Greatest Generation ethics, old-fashioned trust, Yankee ingenuity, and the steel will of our ancestors are all embedded in the meaning of compassionate entrepreneurial leadership.

As individuals and as a nation, we need to remember who we are in order to recover our truest selves if we are to rise from the ashes of our vanity. Our *True South* points to genuine humility, crystal clear ethics, and uncommon entrepreneurial innovation. This greatly needed reformation will extract us from our national morass of the seventeen trillion dollar debt bearing witness to our tragic wanderings. Simply put, compassionate entrepreneurial leadership is the needed catalyst to solving our staggering national debt crisis, our unemployment crisis, our education crisis, our over-40-percent-out-of-wedlock-births crisis, our entitlement crisis, including corporate entitlement during the last two decades, and the ensuing lack of respect of our nation. As Dr. Bill Ellis so wisely stated:

Nothing tottering on the cusp of insanity in leadership and followership can be expected to survive very long. We are the only one of the world's great civilizations still standing. Our present status is shaky. We must do better, a lot better, immediately, if we are to survive as the strong and prosperous nation we have been for 235 years. We must, as a people and nation, make that choice. Nobody else or any other country can decide for us. We need to decide very soon. Our days are numbered.

The conquest of the last frontier on earth, the South Pole in Antarctica as recorded in the explorers' diaries, clearly articulates the effectiveness of compassionate entrepreneurial leadership, the identical leadership qualities of a superlative CEO, educator, politician, clergy, or other important leaders. These *Leadership Lessons from The Ice* are neither mushy (pun intended) nor metaphysical, as they are extracted from rich and compelling data: individual diary entries from a dozen journals. In contrasting the leadership of Amundsen and Scott, as these two determined explorers raced to the bitterly cold icy bottom of the world, one is pulled into the quotidian narrative which pinpoints decisions and circumstances that providentially bring into focus a full color display of both men's leadership ability and shortcomings. Embracing the lessons gleaned from conquering the last frontier on this planet can restore leadership to the greatest nation remaining.

Notes

1. The importance of respect for leaders by the populace as the single most important step to the restoration of national strength is outlined in "Hope and Trust in Troubles Times," a seminal sermon by Dr. Hal Warlick delivered at High Point University.

CHAPTER 4.

AMUNDSEN: A CASE STUDY IN UNIFIED MISSION, CALCULATED STRATEGY, AND ANALYTICAL PREPARATION

Of the many aspects of leadership, strategy and people selection have the greatest impact. Business guru Jim Collins puts it in grade-school terms: "What matters most is who is on the bus and then where the bus is going." In corporate governance parlance, the board of directors is responsible for ensuring there is a cohesive, clearly articulated process to undergird management's strategy.

When orchestrated with skill by directors, strategy impacts the shareholder account; skillful strategy easily pays all director fee costs and then some. We manage things but lead people. Who is on the bus (people selection), the desire of that person to be on the bus (the buy-in Amundsen deemed as important as who is on the bus), and lastly, where the bus is going (mission and strategy) are primary.

AMUNDSEN'S MISSION AND STRATEGY

The mission of both explorers was to be the first to stand on the bottom of the world. Unfortunately, Scott simultaneously embraced scientific discovery as an added objective, with tragically unintended consequences. Unlike Scott's double goals of both scientific discovery and being the first to the South Pole,

Roald Engelbregt Gravning Amundsen

Amundsen's mission was laser focused on his team being the first to reach the South Pole.

Effective leadership hinges on strategy, and Amundsen's ability to think strategically ranks with Napoleon and Alfred P. Sloan. Consistently thorough, Roald Amundsen would have thought strategically about boiling an egg. Furthermore, he knew how to align strategy with pinpoint focus; he knew the importance of buy-in by all members; last but not least, he knew how to effectuate a shared vision by all.

In its broadest sense, Amundsen's strategy was speed, speed, and warp speed. The centerpiece of his elegant strategy was to hold to an absolute minimum the amount of time the Norwegian explorers were exposed to the brutal polar weather each day. To achieve speed, Amundsen combined the use of dogs and skis for the expedition. All in his crew could ski both downhill and cross-country. Aware that dogs pulling sledges and men on cross-country skis could be made compatible in setting a pace, Amundsen believed that man-hauling was much too slow, in addition to being abjectly torturous. Substantially more calories are required for man-hauling; extra food adds noticeably to sledge weight. Weight reduction was a key to his mobility.

Explorers had used dogs before; Norwegian explorer, Nobel Prize–winning statesman, and father figure to Amundsen, Fridtjof Nansen, made the original discovery that the natural gait of dogs pulling a sledge matched that of a cross-country skier. But what about the unsolved conflict that dogs sprint with frequent rests, while cross-country skiers traditionally prefer a long, uninterrupted rhythmic effort? With the advent and subsequent perfection of cross-country skiing in his homeland of Norway, Amundsen recognized the adaptability of humans versus the rigidity of instinct natural to dogs. He knew not to force animals into human patterns, so his dogs set the speed and pace for the explorers on skis to follow.[1]

Pace was sacrosanct to Amundsen even in foul weather. He elevated pace each and every day from a tactical element to a key piece of strategy. How did pace become so important to his leadership strategy? In 1905, when Amundsen became the first ever to navigate the Northwest Passage from the North Atlantic Ocean through the Arctic Ocean to the Bering Sea, he came upon the nearly unspoiled Netsiliks (a band of Inuit Eskimos). Even though they were primitive, Amundsen knew from Nansen and Sverdrup that they had much to teach him, and he viewed the Netsiliks as cultural equals. Amundsen lived with them for a full year, learning most of their secrets gathered over the centuries.[2] Among those secrets was the careful pacing that kept men and animals within their capabilities. Amundsen's wise pacing avoided the limits of endurance; pacing made way for all-out full speed during their intense workdays. Nothing illustrates Amundsen's iron will commitment to setting pace better than his behavior just before they reached the pole. With only fifteen miles remaining, despite not knowing whether Scott was potentially ahead of them, and even with the adamant appeals of his companions to travel onward, Amundsen refused to disrupt his pace. Wait until tomorrow. Take things in stride.

It was also from the Eskimos that Amundsen learned that careful monitoring of exertion prevents too much sweating, an anathema in coldness. Perspiration reduces insulation; it overtaxes man and animal. Amundsen rested the dogs every hour, which meant that the explorers on skis rested every hour. Only so much effort was expended each day—no more than six hours of exertion. The remaining eighteen hours of each day were devoted to sleep and rest in the tent, shielded from the brutal elements. Every scrap of mental and physical energy was preserved. To repeat, pacing meant less exposure to the cruelty of the earth's harshest climate; pacing kept mind and body intact; pacing insured freshness for the next day's work—worthy lessons for all in leadership.

Amundsen remained faithful to this strategy until near the very end of his return trip. When he and his Norwegian team reached the flat Ross Ice Shelf after the ten-thousand-foot descent down Axel Heiberg Glacier, he abandoned his original regimen of sixteen miles a day, allowing his remaining eleven dogs to go for as long as they could without injuring themselves.

On January 25, 1912, Amundsen with his four men, eleven dogs, and two sledges arrived safely at their home base,

Framheim, on the Bay of Whales, Antarctica. They had traveled seventeen hundred miles in ninety-nine days at an average pace of almost seventeen miles per day. Amundsen and his loyal team had executed perfectly on his strategy of speed, thus defying the arrow the ice aims at every man's heart. Not only did this courageous band of brothers triumphantly return home in perfect health, they actually gained weight on the trip!

On New Year's Day 1912, Scott made his final push to the pole, as Amundsen's team flew unseen past the British headed in the opposite direction about 100 miles over the horizon to east, almost close enough to wave, but not quite. Scott's men were beginning to starve, even then, with 950 miles of torturous man-hauling remaining.

So, Amundsen's strategy paid off handsomely. It produced victory. It also ensured life. Amundsen could only hope that Scott would return safely. One week after their return to Framheim, Amundsen and his men boarded their trusted triple-masted schooner, the mighty *Fram*, and left the Bay of Whales. As soon as they reached the island of Tasmania southeast of Australia, the first question from Amundsen was to inquire about the welfare of Scott. No word had been received.

From Hobart, Tasmania, Amundsen sent cables on March 17, 1912, to Norway's king Haakon VII, Don Pedro Christophersen, a major investor in the expedition, and his brother Leon, announcing the news of their success. "The Whole World has Now Been Discovered!" was trumpeted from newspaper headlines all over the world. Like a composer arranging the notes of his musical score, Amundsen was about orchestrating success for his team to do what they had set out to do. Reaching the finale was his best reward; being an international hero was not his objective. Likewise, the few great humble CEOs in the world today are about their people, their management, and the shareholders of the company—not big ego, not entitlement, not fame and fortune. Amundsen was a first humble hound a century before the term was introduced.

SECOND THINGS SECOND: PEOPLE SELECTION

Leader selection is most important, followed by the leadership cadre, in close second.

Jim Collins teaches that who is chosen to ride the bus is more important than where the bus is going because the bus must change directions and make route adjustments many times. Amundsen understood that a key facet of people selection is compatibility, and he knew the extreme importance of attitude, as the explorers would be constantly together in close quarters for more than a year. To this, he wisely injected a new critical question: Does this rider really want to be on the bus? The diaries show that while picking the riders is certainly the critical first step, total buy-in by the riders is also an absolute necessity.

Strategy is the double trump card. Amundsen's diaries show that he substantially enhanced his strategy by handpicking each man for his ability to work in close quarters with other teammates in addition to their critically important experience and skills. Additionally, his men were totally committed, with the unfortunate exception of Hjalmar Johansen, whom Amundsen only admitted at the insistence of his mentor and sponsor, Fridtjof Nansen. Nansen held the sole power to assign the mighty *Fram*, the most famous ship in the world up until the *RMS Titanic* was put to sea on March 31, 1911. Even though Norway had legal title, Nansen was the de facto owner of the *Fram*, and Amundsen well knew that procuring such a ship for the polar expedition stood as a major prize in the seafaring world.

At Nansen's urging Amundsen reluctantly agreed to take Johansen, but as time would tell, Johansen, who had extensive experience exploring with Nansen, was nevertheless lacking in compatibility. When Amundsen and his men initially left base camp to set out for the pole early on September 8, 1911, and were forced by bitter weather to make a hasty retreat back to camp, Johansen publicly dressed Amundsen down at breakfast the next morning. Johansen said and recorded in his diary, among other things: "I don't call it an expedition. It's panic."

From there, he launched into a tirade against Amundsen's entire leadership of the expedition. As far as the events of the previous day were concerned, most of the men agreed with Johansen up to a point, but there was a horrified silence after Johansen's openly rebellious diatribe. Johansen was sorry almost as soon as his rash words escaped his mouth. Reflecting what the others thought, fellow crew member Bjaaland, in an extraordinary moment of heavy followership, noted that Johansen's words were simply . . . "best left unsaid."

In Amundsen's mind, Johansen's outburst was tantamount to mutiny. His authority had been blatantly challenged. Personal feelings aside, this was calamitous in an isolated community, where teamsmanship was life itself:

> The gross and unforgiveable part of [Johansen's] statements is that they were made in everybody's hearing. The bull must be taken by the horns; I must make an example immediately.

Johansen's serious drinking problems had left him unstable. Amundsen, even had he felt inclined, could not afford sympathy. For the good of the expedition, he had to reestablish command as quickly as possible. Johansen, as the old and experienced polar explorer, was a particular danger to their team because, as fellow crewman Bjaaland recorded in his diary, Johansen "could intrigue with the others during the journey and everything would grind to a 'halt.'"

Amundsen began by affecting to leave his outburst unnoticed, addressing himself instead to his companions with an explanation of his actions. The next day, Amundsen announced that Johansen, instead of going to the pole, would travel eastward on a subsidiary mission *under* Lieutenant Kristian Prestrud toward King Edward VII Land. During the evening, Amundsen called his men one by one into the kitchen, where, under an oath of secrecy, he asked for and received a declaration of loyalty. The expedition to King Edward VII Land was not solely punishment for Johansen; it was mainly insurance against failure.

There is no question that Johansen's insubordination did and would have continued to poison the atmosphere in the race to the pole. Even though this episode was the worst crisis in Amundsen's career, his men's all-important cohesion had now been reestablished. His handpicked team (with buy-in) coalesced, eventually winning the grand prize of all terrestrial exploration.

Because all five explorers who made the ninety-nine-day sprint to the pole were experts in skiing, dogs, dog handling, and navigation, the entire journey was a study in heavy followership with each expert moving with fluidity from follower to leader and back, sometimes in short minutes. All understood that Amundsen, the light leader, had the last word. These five explorers easily made up for the unfortunate selection of Johansen.

Adolf Henrick Lindstrom, a crewman whom Amundsen especially admired and on whom he greatly depended, was a particularly wise choice. His positive attitude and jovial spirit as a counterpoint to Amundsen's incredible wit were so important to the Norwegian brothers in the long hours spent at their cramped quarters with the daily grueling monotony: packed snow, glaring sun, same dogs, same food, and same companions. Amundsen knew that informal leaders like Lindstrom—a cook, no less—are crucial. Lindstrom had already proven his value in breaking tensions and building comradeship in the many months together with Amundsen and the crew when they navigated the Northwest Passage in 1903–1905. Having been the foil for Amundsen's elevated humor, this true unsung hero's name should be symbolically etched at −90°.

AMUNDSEN'S ANALYTICAL PLANNING

Amundsen was fanatically detailed in his planning. He researched polar exploration extensively, and as noted previously, he embraced the many lessons learned from living with the Eskimos in his meticulous preparation: He reduced sledge weight, learned diet control, and adopted the wearing of animal clothing, most notably wolf skin anoraks of Netsilik design. In contrast, Scott's men used Burberry™ cloth windbreakers.

A particularly astute aspect of Amundsen's planning was his selection of the site for their home base: He wisely established base camp at the Bay of Whales, sixty miles closer to the South Pole than Scott's base, which further lessened the days of exposure on the ice, enabling them to complete their trek before the coldness became unbearable. Their base camp, Camp Evans, was on the ice shelf four hundred miles east at the edge of the Ross Sea, giving Amundsen a sixty-six-mile round-trip advantage. This reduction in distance more than offset the risk of ascending virgin Axel Heiberg Glacier rather than travelling the expected route up Beardmore Glacier, which Shackleton had marched up to reach the plateau in 1908. Not encroaching on the prior British exploration and base camp at McMurdo Bay appealed to Amundsen's sense of fair play. The consequent sixty-six-mile bonus added significantly to his strategy of speed to minimize exposure to the brutal weather.

After determining their base camp location, Amundsen calculated and recalibrated depot drop-offs and caloric intake like a seasoned bean counter. Before the dark of the Antarctic winter set in, in 1911, the Norwegians set up seven supply depots along their route to the pole, much deeper south than the Englishmen. (The Norwegians' closest depot to the pole at 82°S was 170 miles farther south than Scott's at 79°29' S.) Amundsen depoted a total of three tons (3,048 kilograms) of food with ample fuel, three times more than that deposited by Scott. A real key was that Amundsen had the foresight and knowledge to store seal meat with blubber attached at these depots, to ward off dreaded scurvy. Additionally, Amundsen and his men protected their all-important fuel supply by soldering and brazing all of their paraffin cans to insure against leakage, the necessity of which was tragically illustrated by their British counterparts. A final important precaution was his methodical placement of well-marked, highly visible cairns along the trail, with flags arranged perpendicularly at one-mile intervals, a measure which effectively enabled them to keep pace and travel even in blizzard conditions.

A brilliant, albeit abhorrent, aspect of Amundsen's focused planning was to eat their huskies en route; his immensely difficult decision is viewed as ungentlemanly, even cruelly barbaric, especially in British minds to this day, but it saved his Norwegian backside. This is an example of the survival motivation before the conception of Maslow's "Hierarchy of Needs" in 1970. Amundsen's decision was brilliant in terms of weight reduction of food supplies and sheer speed, which therefore translated to less time exposed to the elements.

Amundsen's careful planning is further illustrated in the fact that he predetermined that on the return trip from the pole, their travel would be at night to avoid snow blindness. Additionally, he ingeniously figured that with strong prevailing northerly winds, sails could be attached to the sledges, so this is exactly what he did on December 17, 1911, after rounding the pole and heading north.

Several more tactical, but nevertheless highly important, details contributing to the expedition's long-term success are that the Norwegians devised tent floors to protect the men from sleeping in water during occasional snowmelts, which occur even in Antarctica. Their goggles were also reconfigured with side slits to prevent the lenses from fogging, long before this design became common as it is today on every ski slope. A final aspect of Amundsen's careful planning is that he and his team spent untold hours modifying their skis and Finneskos for optimum performance and durability while traveling in the fiercest possible terrain.

While Amundsen thought tactically about every detail, Scott had a logistical plan but not a robust strategic plan for capturing the pole. Like a few humble CEOs of modern times, strategy wonks like Amundsen, using light leadership/heavy followership principles, win for all stakeholders. In the hundredth anniversary of these leadership lessons from Amundsen, as comparisons are made between the explorers' circumstances, alternatives, decisions, actions, and results, Amundsen emerges as the effective leader and settles that the ability to think and plan strategically (and situationally when planned strategy fails) is the most important leadership quality.

Notes

1. This following vignette from *The South Pole, Volumes 1 and 2*, by Roald Amundsen, speaks to his love of his dogs as well as his insight into the Alpha Dog. According to Amundsen, with dogs it is simple: All defer to the strongest of the strong. The vignette is also representative of Amundsen's writing style.

   > There can hardly be a more interesting animal to observe, or one that offers greater variety of study, than the Eskimo dog. From his ancestor the wolf he has inherited the instinct of self-preservation—the right of the stronger—in a far higher degree than our domestic dog. The struggle for life has brought him to early maturity, and given him such qualities as frugality and endurance in an altogether surprising degree. His intelligence is sharp, clear, and well developed for the work he is born to, and the conditions in which he is brought up.... Among themselves the right of the stronger is the only law. The strongest rules, and does as he pleases undisputedly; everything belongs to him. The weaker ones get the crumbs. Friendship easily springs up between these animals—always combined with respect and fear of the stronger. The weaker, with his instinct of self-preservation, seeks the protection of the stronger. The stronger accepts the position of the protector, and thereby secures a trusty helper, always with the thought of one stronger than himself. The instinct of self-preservation is to be found everywhere, and it is so, too, with their relations with man. The dog has learnt to value man as his benefactor, from whom he receives everything necessary for his support. Affection and devotion seem also to have their part in these relations, but no doubt on a closer examination the instinct of self-preservation is at the root of all. As a consequence of this, his respect for his master is far greater than in our domestic dog, with whom respect only exists as a consequence of the fear of a beating. I could without hesitation take the food out of the mouth of any one of my twelve dogs; not one of them would attempt to bite me. And why? Because their respect, as a consequence of the fear of getting nothing next time, was predominant. With my dogs at home I certainly should not try the same thing. They would at once defend their food, and, if necessary, they would not shrink from using their teeth; and this in spite of the fact that these dogs have to all appearance the same respect as the others. What, then, is the reason? It is that this respect is not based on a serious foundation—the instinct of self-preservation—but sim-

ply on the fear of a chiding. A case like this proves that the foundation is too weak; the desire of food overcomes the fear of the stick, and the result is a snap.

2. Amundsen's journals record the prevalence of bigamy and wife swapping. The women were described as "absolute beauties, rather small but shapely."

CHAPTER 5.

SCOTT'S MISSION, STRATEGY, AND PLANNING

While both Robert Scott and Roald Amundsen were extremely experienced and proficient explorers, their race to the South Pole clearly illustrates how Amundsen's unified mission, strategic vision, and analytical planning loom large on the leadership horizon, casting a starkly defined shadow over Scott's diluted mission, flawed strategy, and negligence in planning.

SCOTT'S DOUBLE VISION AND MISSION

The stark contrast between the modi operandi of these two leaders is evident throughout their diaries. As stated earlier, Amundsen's focus was trained on one mission: to be the first to reach the South Pole. Rather than seeking personal glory for accomplishing his mission, he simply wanted honor for both his country and his fellow explorers.

Scott, on the other hand, embraced the dual mission of scientific research in addition to vying for the pole. Not surprisingly, the added scientific goal significantly encumbered Scott's mission, vision, strategy, and planning. Knowing how relentlessly the ice stalks her prey, one does not need to look far to see how this scientific mission hung onto the British party's ankles like dead weights in their pursuit of the pole.

The sledges were loaded with cumbersome scientific gear, sapping precious time, energy, and resources, throughout their expedition. A simple example of their double mission's effect is that on the return trip down Beardmore, Scott suddenly ordered Wilson to take a side trip to gather rocks to reconfirm that Antarctica was once a warmer home to vegetation and abundant life.[1] Not only was a precious day lost, but also the specimens added thirty-five pounds (16 kg) to the sledge being man-hauled, without furthering scientific knowledge, yet another example of muddled leadership in the face of exceedingly difficult conditions.

That divided aims are an anathema to sound strategy is also clearly evidenced in the unfortunate fact that the scientists Scott included in his expedition were not trained as explorers. One particularly poignant example of the enormity of this mistake is that, instead of sending a seasoned Arctic explorer to rescue Scott and his men, Apsley Cherry-Garrard, an Oxford educated zoologist, was dispatched with Dimitri Geroff, a dog expert, to One Ton Depot in a final attempt to save the late-returning British party in March of 1912. With eyeglass lenses as thick as the bottom of a wine bottle, the ill-prepared scientist and his companion quickly turned back to base camp near One Ton Depot, all the while Scott's returning party was fighting for their lives. Although well intentioned, Cherry-Garrard had no business on this rescue mission, a point made clearer in his diary:

> If only we had travelled for a day and a half, we might have left some food and oil [for the Primus to melt snow into water] on one of the cairns, hoping that they would see it. . . . It will always to the end of my life be a great sorrow to me that we did not do this.

The diaries continue to provide evidence of the crew's muddled vision. While the inclusion of scientists and their attending gear is seen as dead weight in retrospect, at the time, chief scientist Wilson considered the scientific and geographical work to be the *main* work of the expedition, judging from his diary entry: "No one can say it will have only been a Pole hunt. . . .We want the scientific work to make the bagging of the Pole merely an item in the results."

Lieutenant Victor Campbell, First Mate of *Terra Nova* and leader of the group to explore King Edward VII Land, was even more disoriented. He went so far as to record in his diary that the scientific venture to King Edward VII Land was "the thing of the whole expedition...."

Not only did he have the wrong objective, it was even the wrong geography; King Edward VII Land was a side trip, certainly not the expedition's goal. Amazingly, these entries demonstrate the reality that at least two of Scott's high-ranking officers, including his confidant and protégé no less, did not understand the mission. Scott's leadership was a failure in communication and buy-in. Again we see how Amundsen and his committed team's blinding speed trumped Scott's élan, especially élan and improvisation diluted by scientific discovery.

Besides the fact that Scott's raison d'être was scattered in the Arctic wind, his mission was somewhat tainted by his motives. In peacetime, the way to step over other naval officers was through the time-honored British tradition of exploration, as proven by John Franklin and Walter Raleigh.

Scott's self-serving attitude and overly active ego did not go unnoticed by his ever-insightful crewman, Captain L. E. G. Oates, as he wrote in his diary: "But the fact of the matter is that he [Scott] is not straight, it is himself first, the rest nowhere...."

Another illustration of Scott's self-aggrandizing, unfocused mission and vision is that, while Amundsen single-mindedly applied his energies to achieve blinding speed and weight reduction, the Scott expedition busied themselves with taking hundreds of photos[2]—of men sitting down to tea, the icebound ship, Scott's birthday party, ponies pulling sleds, men pulling sleds, men trying to fix the motor sledges, a cook baking bread, Scott in his den, a dog listening to a gramophone (surely not the inspiration for RCA's logo?), one man's sledding rations for a day, and the group standing around the tent Amundsen had left at the pole. Only two pictures were taken on Amundsen's entire trip—both were of his team standing at the pole.

SCOTT'S STRATEGY: *BRUTE MAN-HAULING*

When reading Scott's diaries and all the related literature, it is quite easy to incorrectly conclude that Scott had a multifaceted strategy based on ponies, motor sledges and dogs; however, closer scrutiny of the diaries makes it clear that Scott believed to his core that man-hauling was the sure strategy. To understand the agony of man-hauling, the heroic self-punishment so dear to the heart of Scott and the British public, the comments of Lieutenant H. R. Bowers, easily the most rugged of Scott's explorers, are revealing. Man-hauling was:

> The most backbreaking work I ever came up against.... The starting was worse than pulling as it required from ten to fifteen desperate jerks on the harness to move the sledge at all.... I have never pulled so hard, or so nearly crushed my inside into my backbone by the everlasting jerking with all my strength on the canvas band round my unfortunate tummy.

Yet despite the torturous effects of man-hauling, Bowers remained faithful to Scott's strategy. When Scott announced that ponies would only be taken to the foot of Beardmore Glacier, Bowers recorded in his diary: "I for one am delighted at the decision. After all, it will be a fine thing to do that plateau with man-haulage in these days of the supposed decadence of the British race."

On December 9, 1911, the last of the five ponies were shot, skinned, and their meat cached at a depot aptly named Shambles Camp. Wilson too recorded in his diary his absolute belief in the rightness of brute man-hauling: "Thank God the horses are now all done with and we begin the heavy work ourselves."

The only explorer of the final five who understood that a horse or dog was built to pull heavy loads, but a human being was not, was the horse expert, Captain Lawrence Oates. Furthermore, he knew that pulling a sledge load of two hundred pounds per man sapped vital energy and drastically impacted speed. Yet from the outset, Clements Markham, the Secretary of the Royal Geographic Society of England and Scott's mentor and sponsor, laid down the cardinal rule for the Discovery, Nimrod, and Terra Nova Expeditions: "No skis, no dogs."

Markham was the orchestrator of the wrongheaded groupthink; with the exception of Captain Oates and Tryggve Gran, there was total buy-in by the rest of Scott's men. Thus, without cross country skis and huskies to pull their weight, Scott adopted the use of untested motor sledges and Siberian ponies; when these quickly failed, man-hauling ultimately became his only strategy.[3]

Markham's desideratum, also adopted by Shackleton, matched well with Scott's talents. Scott was a man of prodigious strength. He had endurance and physical prowess "as the strength of ten," as Alfred Lord Tennyson would say. Never grasping the importance of pace, Scott frequently used his colossal strength to force a day's march well past the endurance of others. Such plays havoc on both the minds as well as the bodies of followers.

How did this intelligent group, starting with Markham and the Royal Geographic Society, Shackleton, Scott, Wilson, and Bowers come to believe in brute man-hauling when substantial evidence in books, diaries, and polar travel experiences, as well as Eskimo history, pointed to the efficiency and efficacy of dogs and skis? How did they ignore over one thousand years of history? The English tradition of "toughing it out" under extreme circumstances, along with their undying belief that man can manage nature, clouded their collective thinking.[4] Untethered élan, the hallmark of many British leaders like Lord Nelson, the most revered Admiral of the British Empire, further contributed to this English bravado.

Along with the British reverence for man-hauling, consider their choice of ponies over huskies. It is known that a pony sweats through its hide; in cold weather their sweat turns to ice, frequently encasing their flanks in an armored plate of solid ice.

A dog sweats only through its tongue, leaving the fur dry. When at rest, dogs dig down into the comforting, protective snow. In stark contrast, the pony stands in the brutal cold. Even when blankets are used and snow walls are built (turning explorers into common laborers, sapping their valuable energy), ponies remain quite vulnerable to wind and cold.

The more serious point is that food does not grow in Antarctica, other than a smattering of moss and lichen. Accordingly, large quantities of fodder are required to sustain ponies and must be forwarded as they advance, greatly impeding speed.[5] Dogs are carnivores; seals and penguins were abundant. While ponies cannot live off the icy land, dogs are in their element.

Additionally, unlike dogs, ponies suffer from snow blindness, rendering them unfit to travel in blizzards and foul weather. That dogs are not afflicted with snow blindness is one of the secrets of how Amundsen adhered to his daily sixteen-mile pace, come hell or high water (frozen, of course).

Next, further consider the evidence against the advisability of man-hauling over the use of sledges pulled by huskies. When not skiing, the Norwegians rode standing on the back of the sledge, just as Inuits did for centuries before them, with speeds 50 percent faster than men pulling sledges on foot with ropes tethered to a corset wrapped around the waist. Even though the British burned seven thousand calories a day while in the girdle straining against the cumbersome weight of the sledge, their daily diet intake was only forty-four hundred calories, according to a study published June 29, 2012, by Dr. Lewis Halsey of University of Roehampton in London. This recent finding leads to the unequivocal conclusion that Captain Scott and his team died of starvation. The sun never set on the collective British arrogance that blinded them from recognizing that they could actually learn from backwater Eskimos.

The cohesive naval in-group closed-mindedness couched in terms of loyalty overrode the clear, *compelling* and *proven* superiority of dogs and skis over ponies and man-hauling.[6] Adhering

Only groupthink could concoct man-hauling as the best way forward.

to the British credo of "no dogs, no skis" and the attending conclusion that man-hauling was the best way forward is arguably the most egregious groupthink fiasco in history!

The compelling pressure of groupthink alongside Scott's staggering leadership deficiencies made for a lethal combination resulting in painful death by extreme emaciation. History is never just history. The blame for the death of the five polar explorers is shared among Scott's British predecessors, trickling down from the top starting with Markham and Shackleton and eventually landing squarely at the feet of Captain Scott himself. In truth, Scott's earlier Discovery Expedition and Shackleton's Nimrod Expedition were both near-death misses based on the same faulty British collective groupthink[7] about man-hauling.

SCOTT'S PLANNING: IMPROVISATION

In the proven technique of storing supplies the summer before the following year's march South, Scott planned his depots along his chosen route before beginning their trek to the pole later in the year. The first part of his depot-laying plan was to establish Corner Camp forty-five miles from their home base at Cape Evans. From there, he planned to establish One Ton Depot as the last supply camp at 80° S.

On Monday, January 30, 1911, from close to home at Safety Camp, 77°55', Captain Scott recorded in his diary: "[I] held a council of war... I unfolded my plan, which is to go forward with five weeks' food for men and animals; to depot a fortnight's supply after twelve or thirteen days and return here."

Even historian Roland Huntford, with no background in management or strategy, noted, "This was the first intimation of what was going to happen. Scott had divulged his plans to no one, possibly because, until the last moment, there were no plans to divulge. The result was a frenzy of chaotic activity. Even Wilson had been kept in the dark, and now found himself scurrying around like a private on parade."

Such was the introduction of most of the party to Scott as explorer in the field. (In contrast, Amundsen posted a map of Antarctica at their base camp outlining their assault narrative and intended route up the virgin Axel Heiberg Glacier, and asked for input and comments from all crew members.)

Following their chaotic departure from Safety Camp, Scott's men began hauling supplies south in preparation for their race to the pole the following year. En route to set up their major supply camp, One Ton, at 80° S, their master plan changed. Against the ardent advice of Captain Oates, which Oates passionately defended, Scott ordered his men to turn back at 79°28½'. This was *120 miles* from their home base at Hut Point, whereas the planned depot was 150 miles from home.

Remembering that the elements are explorers' archenemy,

thirty miles on the ice represents a very major alteration in plan; traveling thirty miles takes at least two days when man-hauling, even in optimal conditions. Named One Ton because of the enormous weight of the supply stash, it was to be an oasis of food, supplies, and safety from the elements, a haven that was intended to be two days closer to the pole on their critical return journey.

It was on February 17, 1911, that Scott decided the ponies could no longer face the "incessant southerly drift" and gave the fateful order to turn. With Weary Willie at the end of his tether, Oates vigorously proposed putting the ponies down and marching farther south to 80° as originally planned. Scott refused; meanwhile, all time stood still, silently awaiting the next exchange:

> *Oates:* Sir, I am afraid that you will come to regret not taking my advice.
>
> *Scott:* Regret it or not, my dear Oates, I have taken my decision as a Christian gentleman.

Later Scott explained his misguided decision, as he lashed out in his diary: "I have had more than enough of this cruelty to animals and I am not going to defy my feelings for the sake of a few days' march."

Captain Oates, who was completely appalled by Scott's mawkishness, had been recommended for the highest military honor for valor, the Victoria Cross, for extraordinary bravery in an intense firefight in the Boer War, wherein Captain Fouche of the Afrikaners had asked for an immediate surrender: "Life and private property guaranteed. All prisoners taken after refusal to surrender will be shot," to which Oates replied, "We came here to fight, not to surrender."

As a seasoned cavalryman, he deeply valued his horses, but regarding Scott's plan to turn back in order to save the ponies, he was very clear on the priority of human life over that of horseflesh. He fully understood and respected military rank, but the unsentimental cavalry officer would not yield to Scott on such shortsightedness. However, his protestations were ignored like all opinions other than his own; Scott viewed such counsel as near treason. The spit-and-polish Royal Navy had only one leadership model: the command-and-control of heavy leadership, meaning you do as you are told and hold your tongue. As earlier noted, this is the same gunpowder stirred into the coffee of the groupthink crowd of the Royal Geographical Society. The practice of heavy followership was not recognized in the Royal Navy and certainly was not exercised. Superior insight by lesser rank was forbidden, even if human lives could be saved—end of story.

Scott himself noted in his diary Friday, February 17: "With packing we have landed considerably over a ton of stuff. It is a pity we couldn't get to 80°."

The real pity, of course, is that Scott's decision to locate One Ton thirty miles farther north proved deadly, quite literally. If Scott had heeded Oates's advice, One Ton Depot would have been reached the following year before Oates's thirty-second birthday, March 17, 1912, the day he died in a raging blizzard at minus 32 degrees Fahrenheit. Additionally, if the depot had been established at 80° as planned, it would have been reached before Scott's Last Tent, the canvas shroud entombing Scott, Wilson, and Bowers. In fact, Scott's Last Tent was a full, safe nineteen miles inside where One Ton was originally planned. As in team sports, the lack of execution of the depot-laying plan sowed the seeds of destruction.

This brings us to April of 1911, as winter set in and the sun began to set for the remaining months. All supplies had been hauled to their depots, and the twenty-five British explorers were packed into Cape Evans in what was known as the Tenement. Even though almost laughable in such quarters, the officers were separated from ordinary seamen as if on Scott's former British battleship *Albemarle* engaged in war. A makeshift wall of provision boxes segregated the bluecoats from the officers. Joined by the scientists, the officers ate their meals separately. To

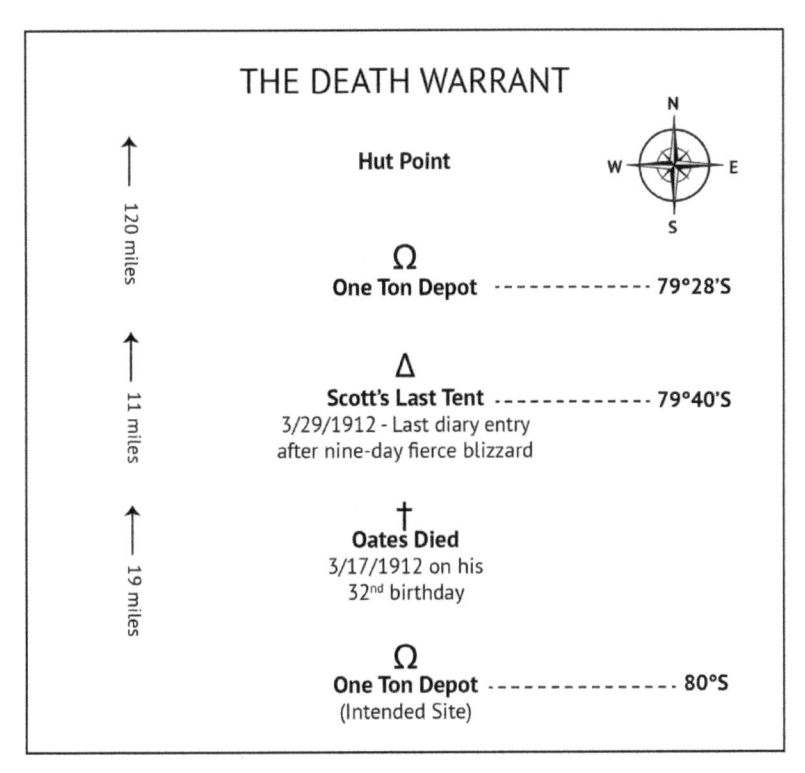

```
                    THE DEATH WARRANT
                                              N
                                          W ⊕ E
    ↑         Hut Point                       S
    |
  120 miles
    |               Ω
    |         One Ton Depot ------------ 79°28'S
    ↓

    ↑               Δ
   11 miles   Scott's Last Tent ---------- 79°40'S
    |         3/29/1912 - Last diary entry
    ↓         after nine-day fierce blizzard

    ↑               †
    |          Oates Died
   19 miles   3/17/1912 on his
    |         32ⁿᵈ birthday
    ↓
                    Ω
              One Ton Depot ------------- 80°S
               (Intended Site)
```

Scott's decision to locate One Ton Depot about 30 miles further north than the intended 80°S proved to be a death warrant.

avoid the tedium of days, which turned to total darkness on April 23, semi-academic lectures were initiated to inform and educate so as to relieve boredom. This was the scene of the darkness of winter with aurora australis pyrotechnics overhead while Captain Scott shed the first light on his plans.

As with his haphazard depot plan devised January 30, 1911, Scott first discussed his plan and alignment of strategy for reaching the pole itself on May 8, 1911, an astounding year and three quarters after the start of the expedition, after the full consequences of not establishing One Ton Depot half a degree further south three months earlier were far from apparent. While Scott outlined his plans for the assault on the pole in the coming season, the men listened in complete silence as he announced that the expedition's timetable and route would be based almost entirely on Shackleton's route retracing the 1908–1909 Nimrod Expedition.

The journey to the South Pole and back, the longest polar trek ever undertaken, was 1,766 statute miles (2,800 kilometers). In three distinct stages, the first 410 miles (660 kilometers) would take the men and ponies across the flat ice barrier to the foot of the Transantarctic Mountains. They would then climb the formidable Beardmore Glacier, which stretches upward for 120 miles (190 kilometers) and rises ten thousand feet (three thousand meters) to the Polar Plateau. The Polar Plateau is relatively flat where they would cover the remaining 350 miles (560 kilometers) to the pole itself.

By this time, Scott had lost all faith in the dogs, and the motor tractors[8] had been a dismal disappointment, which left the ponies as the principal means of carrying supplies on the first stage of the long journey to the Beardmore Glacier, where, ironically, they would be shot. After that, the men, in teams of fours, would drag their own sledges throughout the rest of the journey in winds that at times would reach Beaufort Wind Force Scale 9. The last four yet-to-be-named men eventually chosen to finish the trek to the South Pole with Scott would be forced to man-haul their sledges for almost 1,400 miles (2,240 kilometers) over the worst terrain in the world in sub-zero temperatures.

Scott estimated that the trip would last for 144 days, including twelve weeks on the intimidating Antarctic Plateau where the combination of high altitude—the plateau is almost two miles above sea level—and low temperatures would test their endurance to the very limit.

Scott's plan did indeed test their endurance. In the case of the ones eventually chosen to make the last leg, their limits were defined in death.

Another major planning blunder by Captain Scott was his failure to learn from his own mistakes, the same mistakes recorded in other explorers' written accounts for all to see. The paraffin (kerosene) used to fuel the Primus stoves seeps out of the tin containers in extreme arctic elements unless the containers are hermetically sealed. The Primus, which was the first pressurized-burner, sootless, and wickless stove, was patented in Sweden in 1892 and was universally used by polar explorers to heat food and melt snow for water.

On Scott's earlier Discovery Expedition and in Amundsen's writings, the danger of paraffin seepage in severe polar weather—unless the seams of the tin containers were brazed and soldered—was clearly noted. You would almost be forced to believe that Scott had a subconscious death wish, knowing he had experienced this exact problem on the Discovery Expedition only a few years earlier; nevertheless, inexplicably he did not address it on his subsequent polar expedition. Instead of attending to this important planning matter, Scott continued using the tins with inadequately screwed bungs, which would most certainly leak precious paraffin in severe cold.

It is even more shocking to read Scott's words written in his own hand after his earlier Discovery Expedition concerning the tins from which they drew their oil:

Each tin had a small cork bung, which was a decided weakness; paraffin creeps in the most annoying manner, and a good deal of oil was wasted in this way.... To find on opening a fresh tin of oil that it was only three-parts full was very distressing, and of course meant that the cooker had to be used with still greater care.

Years later, in the sterile fastnesses of the south, oil storage was a matter of life and death. On Friday, February 24, 1912, upon reaching the Southern Barrier depot in the return home from the pole, Scott made this diary entry: "Found store in order except shortage of oil—shall have to be very saving with fuel..."

On this same date, he made yet another note: "Wish we had more fuel... We have the last half fill of oil in our primus and a very small quantity of spirit—this alone between us and thirst."

You can almost hear the words written in the diary moan aloud across the vast icy terrain.

In contrast, having experienced this problem in his successful Northwest Passage in 1905, Amundsen had Hansen make ten tanks holding four gallons each, specially constructed of galvanized iron sheet metal sealed by soldering and brazing all seams to make them absolutely airtight. Amundsen wrote: "If we are to win, not a trouser button must be missing."

Man needs about two-and-a-half quarts (2.4 liters) of water a day in a resting state. While able to live without food for more than a month, humans can only live without water for a little under a week. Working hard at high altitudes man-hauling and in great cold, Scott and his fellow explorers were losing an enormous quantity of liquid through perspiration, so having plenty to drink was a necessity. Scott barely had enough fuel to cook his food, let alone melt snow to produce all the water necessary, so he and his companions suffered greatly from the pangs of dehydration, with its physical battering and unimaginable mental distress. At the same time they were slowly starving, but the pain of thirst is savage: After the body loses more than 20 percent of its normal water content as death approaches, the pain of water deprivation is in the same league as crucifixion.

Scott wrote letter after letter to try to turn his leadership failure to at least heroic defeat.[9] In his letter intended for the public, he attempted to justify himself, find excuses and, regrettably, throw blame on his subordinates, including his words about "the sickening of Captain Oates and a shortage of fuel in our depots for which I cannot account."

True leaders always shoulder blame. Period.

SCOTT'S PEOPLE SELECTION

Besides his equipment problem stemming from the influence of Clements Markham, Scott had a followership problem emanating from the same source: the selection of the members of his expedition was severely burdened by the political intrigues of Markham, who personally persuaded Scott to take on Bowers and also maneuvered Sub-Lieutenant Edward Ratcliffe Garth

Russell Evans into the position of Scott's second in command.

Markham had a complex personality. He was neurotic, vindictive, and insensitive, but when necessary to achieve his own agenda, could be charming and charismatic, underpinned by a veneer of warmth and caring. Adding a further dimension to his complexity, historian Roland Huntford claims that Markham was homosexual even though he was married to Minna Chichester Markham, with whom he fathered a child, Mary Louise, in 1859.

Recognizing the importance of team selection by the leader and its direct effect on team cohesion, it is notable that most of the members of the Terra Nova South Pole Expedition were not handpicked by Scott. This was particularly problematic in the case of Scott's second in command, Teddy Evans, in that CEO succession was a strong likelihood on the monster ice. A rivalry developed between Scott and Evans early on, due to the fact that Evans was only persuaded to go so that he would give up his own aspirations to conquer the pole. Much like Amundsen's second in command, Evans's position was eroded, then eliminated; in Scott's case, he waited until the final eight men of his supporting party were 150 geographic miles from the pole before announcing his plans to send Evans back. Denied the final assault on the pole, Evans and two others embarked on their return to base camp.

Oddly enough, weeks prior to Evans's dismissal, Scott suddenly ordered the sledge party of Lieutenant Evans, Bowers, William Lashly, and Thomas Crean to leave their skis behind and slog on foot for the next three hundred miles, plunging deep into the snow with every step. There is no plausible explanation for this bizarre command unless you understand the management need for others to see their decisions as justifiable and non-arbitrary. Early on, Scott had made up his mind to deny his rival, Evans, the trip to the pole; his irrational order for Evans's team to abandon skis can only be explained by his self-serving desire to wear Evans down and thereby justify eliminating him from the final assault.

Having parted ways with Scott's remaining party, Evans, Lashly, and Crean struggled on foot, fighting for their lives the whole way back to McMurdo Sound. Teddy Evans fully recovered from the near-death experience of scurvy and frostbite on their early return from the pole thanks to the lifesaving efforts of fellow crewmen, Crean and Lashly. Both were awarded the prestigious Albert Medal for saving Evans's life.

Evans had a highly successful career upon his return to England, becoming a war hero at the battle of Dover Straits April 20, 1917. Under Evans's command, two British destroyers defeated six German destroyers to the amazement of the world. The Battle of Dover Straits is in the league with Lord Admiral Horatio Nelson's crushing victory at Trafalgar against overwhelming odds. As an aspiring leader, Evans knew to never let a major career setback deter him from a lifetime of great accomplishment. He was eventually named Sir Admiral First Baron Mountevans, proving that defeat is a temporary condition; it is giving up that makes it permanent. In *A Farewell to Arms*, Hemingway wrote, "The world breaks everyone and afterward many are strong at the broken places." Evans became strong at the broken places and inspires us today to press onward in times of adversity.

It was at the same time that Scott announced the elimination of Evans, Crean, and Lashly that he announced his final bombshell: He would keep Bowers as an extra person on the final leg to the pole, a very major change to their master plan of leading a four-man party. In his usual heavy leadership style, Scott stifled communication with his crew; by now Oates knew the consequences of even a suggestion to "the owner," as Scott was called behind his back. Life in the navy meant that Scott was accustomed to a regime of unquestioning loyalty and blind obedience to orders even when the order was improvisation at its worst. The pitfalls of taking five men rather than the original four would have been evident if Scott had been willing to consult with anyone. The open flow of communication between Scott and his men would have prevented him from casting a blind eye to Evans's and Oates's emerging physical maladies. Scott, Wilson, Bowers, and Crean were by far the most able, the strongest, and the fittest. Crean was a man among men, even above Scott and Bowers in endurance. Not being selected was such a shock (really to all), Crean cried openly. To be Irish is to know sooner or later the world will break your heart. On a final note, this dream team should have been tentatively selected at Camp Evans and given light duty until the final assault on the pole. They all would have lived!

Scott's new diary entry, increasing by 25 percent the number of men for the final charge to the South Pole, spelled their doom: "Ages: Self 43, Wilson 39, Evans (PO) 37, Oates 32, Bowers, 28. Average age 36."

Scott, ably assisted by Bowers's extraordinary organizational skills, had built the entire master plan around supplies and equipment for teams of four. All the food, tents, gear, cookers, and oil depots along the path of the return journey had been designed into pre-packed units of four. The returning party of three (consisting of Crean, Lashly, and Evans, without the remaining Bowers), did not have scales to weigh food nor a measure for the fuel to take three-quarters and leave a quarter. Another problem on the final assault to the pole was the cramming of five men into a tent designed for four.

At the moment this ill-fated decision was announced, the officers should have considered relieving Scott of his command (Article 184 in U.S. Navy) as mentally unfit. Instead, the officers did not even comment on Scott's order. Not one question. Did they fear Scott's rage more than death? Even though the expedition was not a navy project, were they cowed that Scott had demanded and gotten the entire crew's personal signatures consenting to be subject to the British Naval Discipline Act? Whatever the reason for making this last-minute order for five to continue onward rather than four, such insanely stressful polar conditions no doubt heightened the risk of a making a flawed decision. With his fateful order, Scott drafted and signed their next death warrant.

His misguided decision to add Bowers was compounded by his decision to *keep* Petty Officer Edgar Evans (not to be confused with his ex-second-in-command, Edward "Teddy" Evans) in his final group because of Scott's favoritism toward him. Edgar Evans was an ox of a man with herculean strength to match Scott's ideal of physical prowess. It is all too common a mistake to project large build and Samsonian strength to the inner heart and mind as Scott did, a mindset to which many NFL scouts, generals, board members, and CEOs stand guilty. Scott retained Evans for the final leg of the journey despite his cut to the hand, which had occurred while streamlining the sledges *prior* to his selection. Cuts cannot heal in Antarctica's subfreezing temperatures; to add to the lunacy, Evans also had advanced vitamin C deficiency and was in the early stages of scurvy when Scott picked him for the final dash to the pole on January 3, 1912. Standing by without a word, Dr. Wilson's deafening silence regarding Evans's physical condition demonstrated a stunning lapse of professional judgment.

Needless to say, the big Welsh seaman required more scarce food, a problem further exacerbated by the addition of Bowers. It is no surprise that on their way back from the pole six weeks later, on February 13, Scott described their state as follows:

The worst experience of the trip and gave a horrid feeling of insecurity... In future, food must be worked so that we do not run so short if weather fails us. We mustn't get into a hole like this again...

Slowly suffering from gangrene, in addition to starvation, hypothermia, and scurvy, three days later, on February 17, Taff Evans was the first of the five to die, after stumbling behind the others and slipping into a coma. Scott's remaining crew members at that point were Scott's friend Dr. Edward Wilson, the rugged Scotsman Lieutenant Henry "Birdie" Bowers (nicknamed "Birdie" because of his large nose accentuated by his short stature), and Captain Lawrence Oates.

Army Captain L. E. G. Oates was a bright ray of light in Scott's original crew selection. Originally posted with the Inniskilling Dragoons, Oates served with distinction in the South African War before applying for a post on the *Terra Nova*, an appointment for which he paid a thousand pounds. An experienced cavalryman, Scott chose him for his army background and expertise about horses.

Long before Oates and the remaining explorers began their fateful return from the pole, all nineteen ponies were shot and motorized sledges were abandoned. On their return trip, travelling through blizzard conditions, Oates was suffering from severely frostbitten feet as the explorers weakened from lack of food and fuel. As travelling conditions worsened, Oates realized he could go no farther and asked to be left behind, knowing he was holding up the team. When the other three refused, he struggled onward for another day, but on March 17, 1912, as they were huddled inside their tent during a raging blizzard, in a gesture of total selflessness typical of this true gentleman, Oates bravely made his way out into the raging storm, never to be seen again.

Knowing the details of Captain Oates's tragic outcome, it is instructive to consider that his demise was a very avoidable outgrowth harvested from the seeds of destruction sown the prior season by Scott, during the planning and preparation phase of their expedition.

If Amundsen is atop the lamp stand to show the world the leadership value of clearly focused mission, finely tuned strategy, meticulous planning, and careful people selection, it is from the shadowy void that Scott provides a nearly symmetrical picture, albeit a polar-opposite one, of leadership in all areas. Because of his muddled mission and vision, his ill-advised strategy, his careless planning, his haphazard people selection, and his mercurial treatment of those selected, his leadership lessons are precautionary: a not-to-do list punctuated by obituaries to prove it.

Scott had the talent, the strength, the background, the education, and the financial means to lead his men to greatness; instead, he led them into the agony of man-hauling with snow blindness, non-potable water with no fuel for the Primus stove to melt snow, stinging snow driven by howling wind, starvation, severe frostbite leaning toward gangrene, worn, damp furs in sleeping bags, anxiousness over crevasses concealed by snow or thin sheets of ice, poorly marked depots, the mental suffering contributing to the death of Taff Evans and the stoic, heroic death of Captain Oates, all without expressing a modicum of self-doubt or introspection.[10] Finally, on March 29, 1912, the shared nightmare mercifully faded into darkness as Scott and his remaining men, Wilson and Bowers, succumbed to the siren call of the ice.

Notes

1. In its 450-million-year tectonic history, Antarctica moved to its present position about 100 million years ago when it had a much warmer climate than in modern times. Fossils as far south as 85° at times provide evidence of polar forests. Two dinosaur bone discoveries have been recently made on James Ross Island, an Antarctic peninsula. Many factors caused Antarctica to retreat into a deep freeze with a large ice cover, including the establishment of the cold Circumpolar Current circulating clockwise around the continent preventing warm water from reaching the coast.
2. The famous photographer Herbert Ponting recorded the Terra Nova Expedition in a series of stunning, pin-sharp Antarctic panoramas.
3. Markham's famous directive, "No skis, no dogs," was about the superiority of man-hauling, not a complete ban on skis. Skis were used on all British expeditions for man-hauling sledges.
4. A similar spirit guided the building of the unsinkable *Titanic* and then supplied the ship with far too few lifeboats to hold its passengers if disaster did strike. Just as the passengers of the *Titanic* paid a price for

this sort of shortsighted arrogance, so too did Captain Scott and his four companions.

5. Oates even snuck extra fodder on the *Terra Nova* paid for out of his pocket.

6. In the "Deal B%K" section of the *New York Times*, September 12, 2012, Steven M. Davidoff notes that "boards are inherently behind the curve in decision-making and monitoring the all-powerful chief executive" and follows with an insightful observation about today's business climate, some one hundred years after Markham and the Royal Geographic Society: "American directors largely come from the same class and business background, meaning these people can lull themselves into groupthink where diverse views are muted."

7. A linear thinker could imagine Armageddon based on our inability to learn the tragic lessons from groupthink through Pearl Harbor, the Bay of Pigs invasion, and the Vietnam War.

    Groupthink is problematic in boardrooms today with pale, male, stale directors with identical backgrounds and mindsets from the same prep schools, grad schools, and former CEO ranks. The Swissair (aka "Flying Bank") collapse remains the classic illustration of the problem of groupthink in business, exacerbated in that case study by the reduction of board size eliminating industry expertise.

8. You have got to give Scott credit for his engineering mind that enabled him to see the future of polar travel was snowmobiles; you can, however, fault him for not putting the tractors through their paces and debugging them before leaving. Additionally, he unwisely declined to take Engineer Lieutenant Reginald Skelton, the developer of the motor sledge and first diesel submarine engine, with them on the voyage. And then, there is the last enigma to consider: How and why did he not foresee the problem of negotiating crevasses by these bulky tractors?

9. Using wicks as a writing light, Scott penned his last diary entry March 29, 1912. Other than a few log entries of location by Bowers, the others had long ceased writing diary entries.

10. Twenty-year-old Laurie Oates fathered a daughter as a result of a brief affair with an eleven-year-old Scots girl named Effie McKendrick. In his biography of Captain Oates, Michael Smith concludes that Oates never knew he was a father. Michael Smith, *I Am Just Going Outside: Captain Oates—Antarctica Tragedy* (Spellmount Publishers, 2002).

CHAPTER 6.

POLAR-OPPOSITE LEADERSHIP: ÉLAN, IMPROVISATION AND GUTSINESS VERSUS BLINDING SPEED

A glance at military leadership provides an interesting template through which to view our polar explorers. British navy hero Admiral Horatio Nelson was a flamboyant leader and ferocious fighter who possessed the singular ability to inspire his men by his own courage and confidence. After fearlessly chasing down the French and Spanish fleets at Trafalgar during the Napoleonic Wars, Lord Nelson locked onto the enemies' ships and engaged in hand-to-hand combat. Even though outnumbered in ships and men, Lord Nelson led the attack personally, and defeated the enemy.

Civil War general Ulysses Grant's basic strategy was similar: He was essentially a fighter who took it to the enemy. Unlike Nelson, Grant always had more men and more artillery. As commander of the Union Army, he too was a ferocious fighter known for his unyieldingly aggressive military style.

Like General Grant and Admiral Nelson, Scott was a fearless leader. Although heroic in their shared courage, what these three leaders have in common is their tendency to forge strategy with all-out gutsiness, plenty of improvisation, and of course their signature élan.

On point, we see the dichotomous style carved out by Amundsen that is readily comparable to the gifted commander Confederate General Stonewall Jackson, whose core strategy was to "mislead, mystify, and surprise." Jackson's relentless audacity driven by solid forethought and knowledge is as legendary as his ability to inspire his troops to victory amid towering odds. Similarly, there is General William Tecumseh Sherman, whose core strategy of "total war," taking warfare to civilians, was conceived in a Memphis hotel room in 1860. Although cruel beyond the pale, Sherman's laconic strategy is reminiscent of Amundsen's blinding speed in one sense; like the leaders themselves, their strategy was direct and to the point, focusing on the accomplishment of one goal. Revolutionary War General Francis Marion, the Swamp Fox, also built his leadership strategy of shrewd tactical maneuvering: He repeatedly surprised the British and dashed to the recesses of the southern bogs before the enemy knew what had hit them. These four leaders, Jackson, Sherman, Marion, and Amundsen all developed and executed intellectually aggressive strategy. Of great interest, all four of these leaders in the mastery of strategy eschewed élan and improvisation. None predicated their strategy on zealousness, brute strength, ferocity, or bravery. And most importantly, all four concentrated on protecting the lives of their followers, keeping casualties at an absolute minimum.

TACTICAL BLUNDERS

If Scott had been a better leader, he would not have made the blunders that amounted to death warrants for his men: his failure to execute the depot-laying plan, his order for the other sledge team to depot their skis, his last-minute order to add an extra man to the final assault on the pole, and his failure to seal his paraffin tins.

The difficulty of making good decisions amid stressful conditions cannot be overemphasized. Lacking contingency plans, Scott was forced to make important decisions at the last minute under inordinately difficult conditions.

No leader is perfect at all times, but the ability to adapt to changing conditions, especially those unforeseen in the strategic planning stages, is paramount. It is when things go wrong or unforeseen impediments suddenly develop that leadership skills are tested. Undergirded by carefully considered contingency plans, these high-pressured decisions require perspicacity born of listening to your people, being flexible, reading "situational variables," and then taking appropriate action guided by the wisdom of experience. In other words, solid leadership and elegant strategy require these important skills:

- *Integrative capacity* is an ingrained ability, developed through practice, of drawing together diverse elements of a complex situation into a coherent pattern.

- *Catalytic coping* is the ability to invent multiple creative, effective solutions to problems, then when conditions change, to immediately rethink options and adjust plans accordingly.

Amundsen possessed both the integrative capacity and coping skills essential to construct elegant strategy. This requires an openness and flexibility that comes from humility. Egotism only works if you are a George Patton or an Admiral "Bull" Halsey. Unfortunately, humility is not the hallmark of the vast majority of charismatic leaders. Scott's British Navy command-and-control style derailed all hope for the kind of humility in leadership necessary for conquering the ice.

A LOOK INSIDE

When climbing into the attic of Captain Scott's mind to access his leadership credentials, it would be natural to assume his attic to be tidy and in order. After all, he had captained two British battleships commanding seven hundred men during the era when the British Empire ruled the seas of the world. Additionally, Scott had been named commander of the Discovery Expedition in 1901. In his next command, which was to the same icy continent in 1910 on the *Terra Nova*, he was in charge of sixty-five men chosen from eight thousand applicants, eleven who were experienced polar explorers, most with high military rank and extraordinary scientific credentials. Even though navy records noted mission shortcomings, Scott skillfully embellished his accomplishments in his two-volume autobiography, *The Voyage of Discovery*. Through his highly skillful writing[1] he successfully forged an indelible link of "Scott" with "Antarctica" and elevated his reputation in spite of the shortcomings of the Discovery Expedition. Accordingly, Scott was soon thereafter entrusted to lead sixty-five men on this second expedition to Antarctica.

Scott was a decent person, quite the gentleman and a gifted writer. He was well intentioned, mannerly, faithful, and of high integrity. Likewise, he was a brilliant student, especially in complex math. He had the strength of a gladiator. Scott's bravery when facing death was truly incredible. But, alas, a leader he was not. Leadership flaws can be hidden amid the polished organization of British battleships in peacetime. Similarly, poor leadership qualities can be obscured in large corporations, certainly over the short term, but on the ice flaws are literally and figuratively exposed. Being there is like a business start-up where the results of every decision are instantly telegraphed to all stakeholders. Even George Bernard Shaw later realized that Scott was an inept explorer, telling Kathleen Scott's second husband, Lord Kennet, in 1920 that Scott was "unsuited for the job" and that the expedition ended in the "most incompetent failure in the history of exploration."

To this day, Scott's predilection for man-hauling stands as a metaphor for the leadership style that would be his undoing and is emblematic of the hubris, gutsiness, and self-focused improvisation that stood in polar opposite to his rival. Amundsen's relationship-motivated, brilliantly executed strategy of blinding speed and carefully regimented pace pitted against the forbidding tyranny of the ice is textbook example of compassionate entrepreneurial leadership.

Notes

1. After the *Terra Nova* was firmly anchored to the fast ice off Cape Evans, Scott had the dog teams taking light loads back and forth from the ship to the mustering site for stores; in his diary, he noted the initial meeting between his dogs and the most recognizable of Antarctica's birdlife:

   > The great trouble with [the dogs] has been due to the fatuous conduct of the penguins. Groups of these have been constantly leaping on to our floe. From the moment of landing on their feet their whole attitude expressed devouring curiosity and a pig-headed disregard for their own safety. They waddle forward, poking their heads to and fro in their usual absurd way, in spite of a string of howling dogs straining to get at them. "Hulloa!" they seem to say, "here's a game—what do all you ridiculous things want?" And they come a few steps nearer. The dogs make a rush as far as their harness or leashes allow. The penguins are not daunted in the least, but their riffs go up and they squawk with semblance of anger, for all the world as though they were rebutting a rude stranger—their attitude might be imagined to convey, "Oh, that's the sort of animal you are; well, you've come to the wrong place—we aren't going to be bluffed and bounced by you," and then the final fatal steps forward are taken and they come within reach. There is a spring, a squawk, a horrid red patch on the snow, and the incident is closed.

   This casual diary entry is evidence of Scott's natural ability as a writer.

CHAPTER 7.

FORMATION OF VALUES THEN AND NOW

Tone at the top and values are often dismissed in leadership discussions on the grounds that they are elusive and intangible. The concluding statement of the National Commission on Fiscal Responsibility and Reform co-chaired by Erskine Bowles and Senator Alan Simpson underscores the importance of basic values and tone at the top and the need to address them head on. The report is, perhaps, the most definitive assessment of the Great Recession.

We conclude there was a systemic breakdown in accountability and ethics. The integrity of our financial markets and the public's trust in those markets are essential to the economic well-being of our nation. The soundness and the sustained prosperity of the financial system and our economy rely on the notions of fair dealing, responsibility, and transparency. In our economy, we expect businesses and individuals to pursue profits, at the same time that they produce products and services of quality and conduct themselves well in the process.

Unfortunately—as has been the case in past speculative booms and busts—we witnessed an erosion of standards of responsibility and ethics that exacerbated the financial crisis. This was not universal, but these breaches stretched from the ground level to the corporate suites. They resulted not only in significant financial consequences but also in damage to the trust of investors, businesses, and the public in the financial system.

SCOTT'S VALUE SYSTEM

Scott's and Amundsen's value systems and ethos of ethics directly affected their leadership of the Antarctic exhibitions. Amundsen and Scott reduced the critically important tone at the top to very real consequences: life and death.

Scott's value system was established within the entitlement mindset of the British upper middle class, the ethos of the proverbial British stiff upper lip and the polished perfectionism of the rigid navy system. Pluck had become the mantra for the great island nation. By the turn of the century, the Royal Navy had evolved into the world's first superpower, an empire on which the sun never set. Britain's upper class had become the super class, where position soon became exalted over merit. This elitism was reinforced by the exclusion of the workingman, who had no voice and little hope of advancement in Scott's Britain. The effect of this mindset was evidenced by Scott's condescending arrogance regarding counter-advice, especially coming from a bluecoat.

Such entitlement of the upper class is the antithesis of meritocracy, the passageway to national greatness. Compare this to what is happening in America today: Entitlement has moved from labor unions in the early part of the twentieth century to welfare in the middle of that century and now to the executive class itself in the last twenty-five years, with each entitlement taking on an endlessly expanding life of its own. Keeping the Simpson-Bowles Report in mind, one can understand how money, political clout, and deep-throated voice could erode values and create the out-of-sync tone at the top in Scott's Britain on the eve of its decline as the first world superpower.

More damaging to the formation of Scott's leadership values was the top-heavy structure of the immutable Royal Navy, which in effect greatly discouraged creativity and independent problem solving. To repeat, both Wilson and Oates knew that sending five men rather than four on the final leg to the South Pole was a horrific mistake. No comment was made. Silence. Both remembered well Scott's nearly violent reaction to Oates's very sound advice to move One Ton Depot thirty miles farther south to 80° as planned. All knew that Scott considered sound advice, even advice that would have saved lives, as unforgivable insubordination. As earlier noted, following Oates's advice would have saved everyone's lives, including his own. What a shattering indictment of the Royal Navy's deference to the Commander's voice!

AMUNDSEN'S VALUE SYSTEM

Amundsen's value system was forged on the other side of the North Sea in an entirely different environment. The man destined to be the first to conquer the last frontier on the planet was born into a seafaring family that was directly descended from the Vikings. Amundsen grew up on a cluster of islands at the mouth of Christiania Fjord, home of scores of very industrious sailors and fishermen. The region is a harsh environment with long, cold winters, a place where one doesn't just talk about the weather; day-to-day life is ruled by it. It hardens the character of the hardworking people there who quickly learn to adapt to the forces of nature because they know the futility of fighting it.[1] Growing up in this demanding environment and sharing the sap of the Viking family tree contributed in no small way to Amundsen's success as a polar explorer.

Amundsen's values were also shaped by the strong sense of nationalism that swept Norway when the movement for independence from Sweden reached a crescendo as he reached adulthood. His heroic role models, revered Norwegian explorers Nansen and Astrup, led the charge.

Shaped by his physical environment, national culture, and family lineage, Amundsen emerged as a uniquely determined thinker. He did not sit by waiting for opportunity to knock; he pursued opportunity at every turn. While Scott was training to command a shipload of subordinates, Amundsen was learning the importance of commanding his own destiny by taking charge of his life and circumstances. He did not intend, like many, to simply bump off the walls of life's maze, dutifully accepting its narrow confines.

A look into Amundsen's and Scott's formative years gives fresh perspective on how their inner makeup shaped their leadership at the South Pole.

Notes

1. In the assault on the South Pole in later life, he made nature work for him. For example, on the return, he traveled at night at times to avoid sun blindness and erected sails to take advantage of the northerly prevailing winds. The British, in contrast, were hell bent on proving their toughness by struggling as much as possible against the elements.

CHAPTER 8.

AMUNDSEN'S EARLY YEARS

When it comes to the enduring values needed for life's long journey, those bags are almost always packed in the early years of childhood. Amundsen's Viking lineage was a rich starting place for him. Roald Engebreth Gravning Amundsen—each honored Viking family names—was born on July 16, 1872, to Jens and Gustava Amundsen. The family lived and prospered in the tiny parish of Borge, now part of Norway, for Roald's early childhood.

Jens Amundsen became a ship's captain in 1853 and made a large fortune with his ship, the *Phoenix*, in the Black Sea aiding Turkey, France, and England against the Russians in the Crimean War. The sea provided the livelihood for the entire Amundsen family; Jens's four brothers were also ships' captains, as was their father before them. In 1863, Jens married Hanna Henrikke Gustava Sahlquist and settled in Hvidsten, near the important seaport of Sarpsborg. Forged on the anvil of brutal weather with long, crushingly cold winters and frequent storms, Roald's character was shaped in an environment where he learned the adaptability required for survival and the value of hard work early in life.

With Jens frequently at sea, Roald's mother was unhappy living in the stormy seaport of Hvidsten. In an attempt to ameliorate her melancholy, the family moved to Christiania (later Oslo) with the many activities of a capital city, but what was thought to be simple loneliness over Jen's absences turned out to be a chronic case of self-absorption; despite their change in scenery, her discontent persisted even in the midst of wealth, culture, and city lights. Gustava's selfishness filled the upper rooms of her mind, leaving little space for guiding and nurturing her four sons. Roald, especially, was affected by her remote disinterest. Her sporadic interactions with him amounted to little more than mollycoddling, which was not conducive to garnering the respect of her son. Mount Betty, a small ridge overlooking the Ross Ice Shelf, was named for Roald's nursemaid, housekeeper, and surrogate mother, Betty Andersson. His own mother was not so honored in the many similar naming opportunities.

In stark contrast to his father's love for seafaring adventure, Amundsen's mother was humorless and boring, with little interest in Jens's occupation and broad horizons. Despite being very well off and greatly respected in the community, Jens and Gustava Amundsen had a sorry marriage. When home from the high seas, Jens focused his energies on his family, running the household with orderly discipline like a ship on dry land. His larger-than-life persona inspired an abiding respect and left a lasting imprint on Roald's malleable young mind. It was Roald's strong father figure who later dwelled in his heart and mind as he traveled to the undiscovered, foreboding South Pole, leaving his invisible footprints on the ice. This secure but no-nonsense relationship was the fountainhead of Roald's greatness.

Because Roald was the youngest of his large group of childhood cohorts, he was often teased, bullied, and excluded. While exclusion can leave deep wounds, Roald learned to stand up and fight when necessary, in a way that would have made Eric the Red proud. Being the youngest in the crowd, he became very competitive at an early age, as his older companions taught him the national sports of Norway: cross-country skiing, downhill skiing, and ski jumping. During school holidays, Roald and his brothers often went back to Hvidsten, where they handled small boats, played hide-and-seek in the shipyard, and ice-skated for miles between the islands when the sea hardened. Roald spent plenty of time in the harbor town learning about building and repairing wood-hulled ships from the local craftsmen.

Even though Roald had practical sea training, the emphasis of his family was on education. In Norwegian society, academic achievement was the one way to attain higher social status, something money could not buy. Although Jens Amundsen was a wealthy sea captain with his own ship, he was denied social status because he had never gone beyond an elementary education. Additionally, Jens had only one son who graduated from secondary school and two other sons off at sea without finishing their education, leaving only Roald in school at the age of fourteen. Roald's parents held very high hopes that he would push the family up the social ladder by becoming a medical doctor. However, during his secondary school days, Roald became enamored with the writings of Arctic explorer John Franklin, who introduced him to polar exploration. Subsequently, the courageous Norwegian explorer Fridtjof Nansen inspired him by being the first to cross the Greenland ice cap, a permanent sheet of ice covering most of Greenland's landmass.

On a midsummer's day near his twenty-first birthday, Roald watched from his homeport of Christiania as Nansen set sail on a Norwegian-financed expedition that would take his ship, the mighty *Fram*, through the Arctic Ocean to gather scientific information while attempting to reach the North Pole. Nansen had specially commissioned Scottish architect Colin Archer to design the *Fram* with a rounded hull designed to withstand the crushing grip of the Arctic drift ice. Although Nansen's plan was for the *Fram* to become frozen in ice and let the currents take them to the pole, they did not make it all the way. Then Nansen and Hjalmar Johansen set out from the ship on foot with kayaks and sleds, and by sheer perseverance, set a record for distance farthest north, 272 miles from the pole.

Amundsen was captivated by the 128-foot *Fram*, which was destined to become the most famous ship in the world before the christening of the *Titanic*; little did he know that one day he would set out on the brilliantly designed *Fram* as captain, headed for Antarctica (also with Hjalmar Johansen as second-in-command, at Nansen's urging).

Inspired by Nansen's adventures, Amundsen and three friends later set out on a skiing expedition across Nordmarka, near Christiania. Their trip lasted only twenty hours, but they crossed over fifty miles (eighty kilometers) of difficult terrain with outdated ski equipment. With inadequate provisions and skis, they were lucky to get back alive.

During his university years Amundsen happened to attend a lecture by Eivind Astrup, a polar explorer who accompanied the American explorer Robert Peary on a south-to-north trip across Greenland. With the benefit of hindsight, this lecture became an epiphany: Amundsen was introduced to the valuable lessons to be gleaned from the Eskimo way of life in order to be a successful Arctic explorer. Amundsen fully absorbed that European ways would be of no value in the Arctic; he learned from Astrup that to survive, one had to think, act, and live like the Eskimos who had flourished on ice for centuries. From that point forward, Amundsen began adopting Eskimo ways as his own when travelling on the ice.

In his schoolwork, Roald was a below-average student; he had little or no enthusiasm for university studies, barely scraping by his final examination in secondary school. Nonetheless, as his parents wished, Roald entered the medical school at Christiania University where he later failed his examinations and, following his mother's death in 1893, dropped out to pursue his real ambition: to become a polar explorer in the image of Nansen. The Viking could still hear the call of the polar wild.

Amundsen understood that the path to polar exploration was through experience and learning lessons from more experienced explorers like Nansen and Astrup, because his own skills in skiing as well as seamanship were still somewhat lacking. One of Amundsen's early training regimens was to sleep in the frigid northern wind to inure his body to the cold. Having skied the lowlands of Nordmarka, he turned his attention to mountains west of Oslo, Hardangervidda. With the polar frontier the focus of all his thoughts, it was providential that winter conditions in the mountains were very similar to Antarctic conditions.

Amundsen soon joined Laurentius Urdahl in an attempt to cross the plateau at the foot of Hardangervidda, but they were both beaten back by raging blizzards. Even though Urdahl turned back to return to Christiania, Amundsen refused to accept defeat. Trying anew to cross the plateau, he attacked Hardangervidda again when he was twenty-three, this time with his older brother, Leon. They were defeated in a blinding whiteout on a frigid day in 1896; not a talisman of good luck, yet still showing the kind of wonderful perseverance important to strong leadership. It was by getting slammed hard in his own backyard that Amundsen found direction for attacking new frontiers in his life.

Six weeks later, Amundsen signed on to the sealing ship *Magdalena* to learn the techniques of sailing in the icy waters of the Arctic. On this trip, Amundsen found that the cruel slaughter of seals was beyond anything he could countenance. This profound respect for animal life would later manifest itself in his love for his huskies. He accepted that killing animals was necessary to obtain food and clothing, but in his mind the inhumane slaughter of so many seals was indefensible. In future years, Amundsen did kill animals for food but only when necessary to save his men, in a way similar to Native Americans' value system. (Scott shared a similar angst over animal slaughter, but the diaries suggest it leaned toward sentimentality rather than reasoned concern.)

At the age of twenty-five, Amundsen embarked on a scientific expedition to Antarctica as second officer on the *Belgica* with American explorer, Dr. Frederick A. Cook, M.D., who demonstrated that partially cooked seal meat prevents scurvy, a disease caused by lack of vitamin C. During this venture, Amundsen was the *first* person to ski on the Antarctic continent, and was part of

Antarctica's *first* sledging party. When the *Belgica* became stuck in pack ice, her crew achieved the unintended distinction of being the *first* humans to overwinter in the Antarctic, a hat trick, in sports parlance, of firsts achieved by Amundsen. Even though he was not in command, this expedition is instructive of "heavy followership" by Amundsen, as he frequently encountered situations in which he was needed to move from follower to leader. Just as fluidly, he would resume being an effective follower as the circumstances changed.

Observing Amundsen's earlier learning experiences as they swell to a crescendo, one can easily see why most believe that intensely focused preparation is the reason Amundsen became one of the greatest explorers in history. These early expeditions helped Amundsen conclude that command of the ship and command of the expedition needed to reside in the same person. In 1900, he completed his sea training and gained his master's certificate. In his many excursions seeking to gather crucial experience in exploration, he learned early on to plan for the worst but hope for the best. He learned the importance of contingency planning as a crucial part of strategy; such plans would obviate last-minute decisions while battling the intense hazards of polar extremes. This same ability to think strategically in planning for the worst would eventually keep his band of brothers only minimally exposed to the −40 degree weather and the harshness of many Antarctic storms.

Because of Amundsen's ability to hone in on the important takeaways to be garnered in his early life experiences, Amundsen gradually built up his leadership arsenal. Ultimately, Amundsen would set the high water mark in his brilliant assault in the pole. With his all-encompassing strategy of blinding speed, Amundsen substantially reduced his men's and animals' exposure to the brutal weather, adhered to pace, and avoided the misery of man-hauling. Using relationship-motivated light leadership while eschewing the exclusion he experienced as a youngster, Amundsen conquered the pole. Yes, his years of extreme preparation were important, but it cannot be emphasized enough that strategic planning won the race.

CHAPTER 9.

SCOTT'S EARLY YEARS

Over the years, many a schoolboy has grown up lionizing Robert Falcon Scott, reverently romanticizing his courage, strength, and determination.

Larger than life, Scott stood regally in his full dress as Captain of the British battleship *Albemarle* with its ten thousand tons of expensive ironmongery. Knowing that at the age of thirty-eight, Scott had seven hundred men under his command of the entire Atlantic Fleet as he rose to the position of Chief Executive Officer in January of 1907, who would not be awestruck by his prodigious ascendancy?

To put the might of the Royal Navy into historical perspective, their first dreadnought was put to sea the year before, in 1906. These mighty warships relied almost entirely on their main battery of ten twelve-inch guns for firepower; each turret had its own specially armored magazines for shells. The dreadnought displaced 20,700 long tons, fully loaded. At the time, Britain had more of these "battle wagons" than any nation on earth. The word "dreadnought" instantly evoked fear in the hearts of Britain's enemies.

Many were called, but few were chosen to command the mightiest warships of the Great Empire that ruled the seas. The Royal Navy attracted the strongest of the strong and elevated the very brightest rising stars, with battleship commanders being at

Captain Robert Falcon Scott: A gentleman and a scholar does not a leader make.

the apogee of their high elite—thus completing the lionization of Sir Scott in every young boy's heart.[1]

The groundwork for launching his legendary ascent was laid early in life. Scott was born on June 6, 1868, to John Edward and Hanna Scott at Outlands near Plymouth, England. He had three sisters and a brother; also living with them were nine servants and a relative. While John Scott was the owner of a small brewery passed down through the family, he spent much time as a country gentlemen, gardening in his spare time. Although John remained the final authority, Hannah ran the household, managing the servants, and making most of their major decisions. Her influence on her adoring sons was indelible and deep. She kept an orderly home appropriate for their upper class lifestyle, while keeping a firm watch on her brood.

Young Scott began his education at home with a governess, and at the age of eight went to school with the other children until he was thirteen. Scott's father chose a military career for both his sons: Robert would prepare for a career in the Royal Navy and Archibald would serve in the army; they were given no choice, and they did as they were told. Robert Scott was an excellent student and passed the rigorous examination for officer's training the first time. At age thirteen, he became a navy cadet and was assigned to the training ship *Britannia* to learn the ways of the Royal Navy. Quickly absorbing the navy's highly regimented style, the unquestioning obedience to authority learned in his early years became his marching code, all to the likely detriment of his ability to think independently.

Cadet Scott excelled in navigation, seamanship, and especially mathematics at the Britannia Royal Naval College in Dartmouth. Despite the fact that Scott later emerged as an exceptional writer, Renaissance thinking was not a requisite skill for becoming a naval officer; English and composition were not taught, as it was not deemed particularly important for an officer to express himself well. This repressive intellectual climate ushered the cadets into a narrower way of thinking and operating in their military environment.

Promotion in rank was based on academic achievement alone, an area in which Cadet Scott excelled; he graduated seventh in his class of twenty-six and was rated a midshipman. Interestingly, leadership ability was not even a consideration in the promotion process, so Scott or any other cadet could progress through the ranks without due scrutiny of the leadership skills necessary to command.

Following his studies at Dartmouth, Scott spent four years at sea getting practical experience. After sea duty, he was automatically promoted to sub-lieutenant and sent for further study at the Royal Naval College at Greenwich, where he did extremely well, again finishing very near the top of his class. He was awarded four first-class certificates out of a possible five, which qualified him for further promotion following his mandatory sea duty. Although on August 16, 1889, at age twenty-one, he earned the rank of lieutenant, his professional ascent was not without occasional setback. In August of 1893, after Lieutenant Scott received his first-class certificate and qualified as a torpedo lieutenant, he ran the torpedo boat aground while serving as temporary commander, for which he received a severe reprimand. He was obviously much better at theory than with navigating actual situations, a fact that would become increasingly apparent years later as he led his men to their deaths in the race to be the first to reach the South Pole.

In 1901, at the young age of thirty-three, Scott was named commander of the sailing ship *Discovery* and embarked on his first Antarctic expedition. The Discovery Expedition was organized by the Royal Geological Society for the purpose of scientific research and Antarctic exploration. Noted Anglo-Irish explorer Ernest Shackleton was Scott's third officer, and Dr. Edward Wilson, who would later accompany Scott on the Terra Nova Expedition, went as assistant surgeon. Among the lower deck complement of this expedition were additional members of the future Terra Nova Expedition of 1910: Edgar Evans, William Lashly, and Thomas Crean. Crean joined the expedition following the desertion of a seaman in New Zealand.

Scott returned from the Antarctic a national hero and was catapulted into the exalted heights of British society. He was promoted to captain and showered with numerous titles, honors, and medals, even though this first expedition did not meet some of their desired objectives, resulting in a slight blot on his navy copybook. The navy was forced to dispatch expensive rescue teams to save *Discovery*, which was firmly embedded in ice. During the Discovery Expedition, Scott and fellow crew member Dr. Edward Wilson did succeed in establishing a new record for Farthest South at 82°17', meaning they never got beyond the Ross Ice Barrier. Third Officer Shackleton was not invited to share this distinction of the Farthest South, a slight that was never forgotten and gave rise to an intense, lifelong rivalry.

In 1908, Scott married British socialite Edith Agnes Kathleen Bruce at the Royal Chapel at Hampton Court Palace. The fashionable couple enjoyed a fast-paced social life until Scott's next expedition. Ironically, Kathleen, who fed Scott's ego like a goose destined for foie gras, shortly thereafter had an affair with Amundsen's famed hero, Norwegian explorer Fridtjof Nansen, in a Berlin hotel room, as "Con" Scott (her endearing name for her husband) was marching to his death on the ice in 1912. Nansen later received the 1922 Nobel Peace Prize. A noted cosmopolitan sculptress who trained with Auguste Rodin in Paris, Kathleen was granted the title Lady Scott in 1912. Earlier the same year Robert Scott succumbed to the siren call of the ice, where he remains forever frozen in her icy grasp. He was later immortalized in the stony form of bronze statues sculpted by his artist wife; he stands today in Waterloo Place in London and in Christchurch, New Zealand, bringing his lionization full circle.

Notes

1. Many at the highest level of business understand the axiom, "The skill sets for running a big business are dichotomous from those needed for a small company." Scott was a "big ship" man used to the anonymity of large, multi-layered crews. What was needed on expeditions was a "small ship" man, like the captain of a destroyer, a light cruiser, or even

a submarine, who operated in close contact with his men. The Royal Navy even then recognized the difference and took into account the need for different leadership styles and personalities; they understood that these nearly opposite leadership styles could not be reshaped to morph into one another. Is it surprising that a battleship captain who was viewed by his men as God Almighty could not understand, much less successfully practice, light leadership/heavy followership?

CHAPTER 10.

VALUES: WHERE THE BUCK BEGINS

Even though there is no perfect laboratory to compare leadership strategy and behavior, our controlled variables are: time, terrain, weather, and goal. Further, we have rich data from cross-referenced diaries, stripped of all posturing.

Amundsen (age thirty-nine) and Scott (age forty-three) were vulnerable to the identical extreme environment during the same time period, attempting the same achievement. That is to say, both Amundsen and Scott started their assaults on the pole within days of each other; both faced a round-trip of more than seventeen hundred treacherous miles in an out-of-control environment, frequently enduring temperatures 20 degrees below zero (even during the summer) while bracing against gale-force winds driving the windchill even lower. They shared the exact same dangers with no radio, cell phone, or satellite link to base camp, in an environment where the first leadership misstep is potentially the last.

Keeping this shared experience in mind, witness several of Scott's many very telling comments sprinkled throughout his polar diaries in which he places the blame for their misfortunes squarely on bad luck with weather:

> I doubt if any party could travel in such weather.
> Our luck in weather is preposterous.
> It is really time the luck turned in our favour—we have had all too

little of it.

Yet after all it would be humorous enough if it were not for the seriousness of delay—we can't afford that, and it's real hard luck that it should come at such a time.

All this soft snow is an aftermath of our prolonged storm. Hereabouts Shackleton found hard blue ice. It seems an extraordinary difference in fortune, and at every step S.'s luck becomes more evident.

We could see nothing, and the pulling grew very heavy. At 5:45 there seemed nothing to do but camp—another interrupted march. Our luck is really very bad... but oh! for fine weather; surely, we have had enough of this oppressive gloom.

Worse luck, the light airs come from the north and keep us horribly cold.

No doubt about the going downhill, but everything going wrong for us. Yesterday we woke to a strong northerly wind with temp. −37°. Couldn't face it, so remained in camp...

The fact that Amundsen and Scott were subjected to the same extreme weather is clearly reinforced in Roland Huntford's *The Last Place on Earth*. According to Huntford, both explorers had virtually identical good days to bad days of weather: 56 percent good weather days and 44 percent bad, with the only difference being that Amundsen got his team off the ice earlier, returning to base camp at Framheim on January 26, 1912. Lingering to late March of 1912 was beyond unfortunate. As atmospheric scientist, Susan Solomon, reports in her 2001 book, *The Coldest March*, there was a severe cold snap that month: "Scott and his men struggled through three weeks when almost every daily minimum temperature was a bitter and debilitating 10–20° F colder than what can now be shown to be typical."

While Scott was contemplating his bad luck with the weather, the ice silently swallowed him up, along with his team. In March, as they began to perish, staggering from exhaustion, snow blindness, scurvy, the onset of gangrene, dehydration, and hypothermia, Scott and his men made their final diary entries and wrote letters to loved ones in England to say their fond good-byes. Tragically, the fact that they were still exposed to the cruel polar elements in the singularly miserable month of March in 1912 was due not to his bad luck but to the blind spot of groupthink at the highest level of British leadership over many years, exacerbated by Scott's inept leadership. Given the evenness of the playing field, it was simply not proper for Scott, or any other leader for that matter, to have refused to accept blame for his personal failure which resulted in exposing his men even into March.

The leadership void that precipitated Scott's failed strategy and poor planning is the same void that triggered Scott's arrogant blindness to his own culpability. The crucial role of foundational values in leadership could not be more starkly illustrated than by the absence thereof revealed in these sad diary entries.

CHAPTER 11.

CHALLENGES: POINTING TRUE SOUTH TOWARD LEADERSHIP EXCELLENCE

We have established that wise strategic planning and successful implementation of strategic objectives are the most important markers of entrepreneurial leadership. While the role of strategy is paramount, the essential role of values in leadership cannot be underestimated. It is on the firm foundation of unambiguously focused values that the leader's vision, energy, and authority are rooted and sustained, winnowing the wheat from the chaff in leadership. The essential and all-encompassing arena of values gives substance to compassionate entrepreneurial leadership and illuminates the way forward in today's world. The way forward is paved with ten essential facets of leadership excellence, all of which Amundsen possessed:

CONSISTENCY

Consistency as a leadership trait is misunderstood and underrated. Consistency is the trait that explains how Bill Gates, who was an intellectual intimidator, could lead: He was a consistently hard-nosed cynic, not your best pal one day, a cold fish the next, and then an intimidator the next. Similarly, John J. Brennan is the epitome of leadership consistency. As the Chairman and CEO of Vanguard, with $1.4 trillion under management, he is consistently dull, so dull in fact that you have probably never heard of him. Far from being a leadership negative, Mr. Brennan's employees view his consistent dullness to be an endearing trait. Vanguard's story is made more amusing by the fact that his uniquely dull consistency is extended as a client attribute; because of it, he had no exposure to subprime and structured investment vehicles when the markets crashed in 2008. Who says dull is dull? Another example of the importance of consistency is Steve Jobs, who in addition to being a genius, was considered a real jerk. Even though counterintuitive, being a *consistent* jerk can turn this otherwise unflattering reputation into a leadership plus. The security of knowing what to expect can be of great comfort, even when the expectation itself is not entirely positive!

Likewise, the diaries illustrate the importance of consistency as a leadership trait. Amundsen's moods, personality, and approach did not vary; his teammates knew what to expect. He was a consistent low-key helpmate ready to give guidance in determining solutions. In contrast, Scott was not only inconsistent in his overall approach, but he was moody—sometimes the picture of composure, and then flying off the handle at other times: "He was a kind of Dr. Jekyll and Mr. Hyde, and he had a heavy vein of irrationality in his make up."[1] Birdie Bowers, who had become Scott's dependable right-hand man responsible for keeping the trains on time and sweating the details, reported breaking the thermometer on December 27, 1911. Cracking this very fragile instrument, which in conjunction with the hypsometer gave altitude readings, was hardly Bowers's fault, but Scott's emotional tirade was beyond extreme, as reflected in Bowers's diary entry:

> I got an unusual outburst of wrath in consequence, in fact my name is mud just at present. It is rather sad to get into the dirt tub with one's leader at this juncture, but accidents will happen.

Witnessing Scott's fit of rage against his second most trusted ally is sure to have put a pall on all eight remaining explorers as they slogged southward.

In a study released in September 2011 Google, Inc. examined what employees valued most in a manager. Technical expertise (which can be delegated) ranked last among eight qualities listed in the survey, while staying even-keeled ranked number one, followed by asking good questions, taking time to meet with people, and caring about employees' careers and lives. In summary, the Google study validated that consistency is the most valued leadership trait. Had CEO Larry Page read the polar diaries, it would have saved them the expense of consulting fees.

HUMILITY

As previously noted, Amundsen was the forerunner of the humble hound. In his now famous April 8, 2010, *New York Times* editorial, David Brooks coined the term, asserting that many of the reliably successful leaders combine "extreme personal humility with intense professional will."[2] In sharp contrast, Scott was the forerunner of the imperial CEO. Glomming onto the British system of fast-tracking navy rank via exploration during peacetime, Scott allowed his personal ambition for promotion to eclipse his interest in the well-being of his fellow explorers. After Scott's blazing row with Oates's close friend, Cecil Meares, Oates penned the following in his letter home October 31, 1911: "Myself, I dislike Scott intensely and would chuck the whole thing if it were not that we are a British expedition and must beat these Norwegians."

And here at the close of his letter we are reminded of Oates's haunting words that shock our sensibilities still a hundred years later, speaking virtual volumes about Scott's lack of humility: "But the fact of the matter is that he is not straight, it is himself first, the rest nowhere . . ."

Perusing expedition photographs showing Scott seated regally at the head of the table and Amundsen sitting among his band of brothers offers a stark portrayal of contrasting leadership. With idiomatic clarity, these images paint a visual definition of both true humility and the unfortunate lack thereof.

Where and how did Amundsen develop such inner humility and compassion for his fellow explorers? How did he come to understand that real power is never external, but instead always comes from within?[3] In the way similar to all leaders in training who have sorted it out throughout civilization, beginning with Moses: Humble leadership comes like little cat feet over many experiences through the years, sometimes during the day but often at night while reflecting on the day, bit by little bit, learning from missteps, and building on positive outcomes. Leadership textbooks, seminars, and biographies of great leaders are only suitable to highlight principles. There is absolutely no substitute for on-the-job leadership training each and every day of one's life; even then, the vessel of leadership lessons to be learned is never filled, no matter how experienced, no matter the length of service.

With shareholder value destruction by celebrity CEOs, the heightened status of humble-hound leaders—like Bill Johnson, CEO of the Tennessee Valley Authority; Ellen Kullman, CEO of Dupont; Doug Oberhelman, CEO of Caterpillar; Bob Iger, CEO of Disney; David Rubenstein, managing director of Carlyle Group; Alan Mulally, CEO of Ford Motor Company; General Martin E. Dempsey, chairman of the Joint Chiefs of Staff; Geoffrey Canada, educational pioneer; and Allen Parker, chairman of Cravath, Swaine & Moore—is even more evident today.

As with these respected leaders, Amundsen's leadership credo was light leadership/heavy followership, which requires confident humility. The blending of these three attributes—light leadership, heavy followership, and humility—fosters the highest level of teamsmanship essential for life's journey toward *True South*. Amundsen excelled in inspiring people—in capturing hearts, minds and souls—with the same deft aplomb as he skied to the pole at warp speed.

Most great enterprises are the product of cohesive teams, woven together with light leadership. It is humility that breathes life into light leadership; light leadership is impossible without it.

The single all-powerful CEO is a myth; it is always the cohesive team that wins the race.

The concept of servant leadership, with the imagery of washing the followers' feet, sometimes goes hand-in-hand with light leadership. However, Amundsen wisely knew that tough empathy occasionally had to take precedence over servant leadership and established his boundaries accordingly, reserving the attitude of servant leader for instances where tough love was not required. Even though he washed out as a medical student, Amundsen managed to learn the value of chasing out pathology in pursuit of wholeness. More importantly, he also knew that humility doesn't have to be hung at the door leading to tough empathy: The need for humility is unchanging in all things big and small, which hearkens back to the subject of consistency.

Amundsen led by inspiration and deeds. Scott led by exhortation and intimidation. Amundsen asked for input. Scott asked for strict obedience to orders.

AUTHENTICITY

We have determined that inspired leadership requires several traits working in tandem; not all, by any means, but certainly more than a couple. Scott had education, writing ability, social standing, personal decency, and charm in this leadership column, none of which are leadership traits; Amundsen had each of the ten leadership traits to some small degree, with the first three extremely well developed: consistency, humility, and authenticity. With that bolted to the mind, the diaries teach the uncommon common sense that any aspiring leader is DOA if not authentic. That is the first commandment of true leadership. Forgive the stab at humor, but authenticity cannot be faked.

Amundsen was authentic to the core. He was uniquely "comfortable in his own skin," lacking guile and full of sincere compassion for his band of brothers. In his growing-up years, Amundsen managed not to develop the overblown ego and shallow veneer characteristic of many achievers. He was a practitioner of light leadership/heavy followership even in his early endeavors. His respect for his followers and willingness to let them take the leadership reins in their specialty were born of authenticity and confident humility.

Leadership habits and traits can never be mechanical. They must be a fully absorbed and digested part of the executive's personality, learned to the point of being truly authentic. That is why the thousands of "recipe" business books are snake oil for the most part, and today's $5,000 seminars teaching cookie-cutter leadership are fraudulent per se. Amundsen's well-developed traits were not learned in a classroom or seminar. Like all leadership traits, men and women learn them through unwavering attentiveness over a lifetime of committed watching, listening, and waiting in daily heavy followership experiences, beginning at Mama's knee.

LAUGHTER AND HUMOR

"Against the assault of laughter nothing can stand." —*Mark Twain*

A natural sense of humor is a fabulous asset in the leadership world, a place where taking oneself too seriously is a virtual epidemic. The ability to laugh, especially about oneself, is an immediate ticket to rise above the inevitable complexities of life, or as Milton Berle so famously noted, "Laughter is an instant vacation." Like attitude, laughter spreads goodwill horizontally in every direction and can turn darkness to light in the blink of an eye.

With the help of Lindstrom, the cook, Amundsen turned levity and revelry into a leadership art form. Lindstrom had much to offer the crew in the way of expertise; providentially, beneath his celebrated wit and clownishness, he was a very experienced polar cook who understood the importance of good nutrition, having earlier sailed the *Gjoa* with Amundsen. Even before it was known that vitamin C deficiency was the cause of scurvy, Lindstrom recognized that undercooked seal meat thwarted its onset. He further recognized the nutritional value of whole wheat versus

English white bread. Lindstrom's specialty was buckwheat cakes topped with whortleberries and cloudberries, both traditional Norwegian antiscorbutics. However, of equal importance to providing expert nutritional sustenance, Lindstrom and Amundsen often nourished the crew with a good belly laugh, the best soul food of all.

One of many examples of their lighthearted comedy occurred at their base camp at Framheim. Lindstrom generally set his alarm clock to awake at six-thirty in the morning, but occasionally it would accidentally ring at six-thirty in the evening as well, sounding much like a telephone. It was Amundsen's idea to tell Lindstrom to answer it, but without missing a beat, Lindstrom followed suit by acting out a phone conversation for all to hear, and then with a perfectly straight face, retold the made-up conversation to Amundsen, creating an air of revelry for all to share. Recorded in Amundsen's diary is his telling of it:

> And then, we both laughed and enjoyed ourselves like children. The odd thing is that this happened three evenings in a row, always with the same result—amusement.

Amundsen arranged the last lap from the pole to Framheim to arrive at four o'clock in the morning on January 26, 1912, ten days ahead of schedule. Ever the prankster, he began the last leg of their ninety-nine-day journey by quietly unhitching the eleven dogs, and then he stealthily crept into the hut where Lindstrom, Stubberud, Prestrud, and Johansen lay sound asleep. He woke them up, startling them all with a rollicking order for Lindstrom to fix his morning coffee, jovially clucking: "Get up, boys, it's the first cuckoo of spring."

Innocence, good food, and humor are critical tools for combating cynicism and pessimism. They serve as some of the smooth stones needed for slaying the internal giants of negativity and world-weariness.

Both Amundsen and Scott understood the team value of providing favorite food and drink on special occasions, but Amund-

Banquet at the hut at Cape Evans, McMurdo Sound: Scott presides at the head of the table on June 6th 1911 for a southern midwinter birthday celebration at their base camp at Cape Evans. Unknown to his men, Atkinson (far left), Meares, Cherry-Garrard, Oates (standing), Taylor, Nelson, Evans, Scott (at head), Wilson, Simpson, Bowers, Gran (standing), Wright, Debenham, and Day, Scott's 43rd birthday would be his last.

sen especially excelled at building esprit de corps through revelry. Food and fun served as powerful tools used to entice, comfort, reward, and build collegiality along the shared journey, a great lesson for leaders of every stripe.

If laughter is good for the soul, it is even better for leadership; never underestimate its power in the arsenal along the road to leadership excellence. It is key.

LISTENING WITH AN INTUITIVE SENSE

"Were you talking when you should have been listening?"
—Tough Empathy from The Strolling Professor, *William R. Johnston*

One rarely learns anything of value while words are leaping

off the tongue; however, the opposite is true when a person is listening. Most people are naturally inclined to love "hearing themselves talk" and erroneously assume the rest of the world is similarly enamored. As counterintuitive as it may seem, real listening requires far more energy, focus, and selflessness than talking. In fact, true listening requires more focused energy than practically any leadership discipline.

Silence is a gift; it is the creation of a space for others to step into and let the listener know what is important to them, what is on their mind, and what their needs are. An attentively intuitive listener can not only selectively discard the nonrelevant information, but also read the speaker to glean important information beyond the spoken word. This sort of listening requires staying absolutely in the moment, not thinking back or rushing ahead. Listening is a learned skill, and it requires the listener to stop completely and devote all senses to take in the moment at hand.

> To watch his woods fill up with snow.
> My little horse must think it queer
> To stop without a farmhouse near.
> —from *Robert Frost*, "Stopping By Woods on a Snowy Evening"

Just as stopping in the woods on a snowy evening to watch and wait may seem like a questionable use of time, stilling the busy rush of daily life long enough to get a clear sense of what is being said often fades off the radar in daily priorities. However, wise leadership requires far more listening than talking. The silent space after the struck note is essential to the musical composition. It is in reality when your senses fully engage.

Amundsen made himself available to his men in a way that allowed for real communication. Besides being an empathetic leader, he was an excellent sensor of the situation at hand. He had the necessary insight to assimilate and interpret soft data by sniffing out the signals in his surroundings to instinctively understand the situation without needing hard evidence to spell it out for him. Amundsen fully sensed the feelings and concerns of his men throughout their amazing sprint to the pole. His refined sensors paid off; his men adored him. Amundsen was an intuitive leader who inspired others to share impossible hardships with him.

Meanwhile in polar-opposite fashion, Scott's unwillingness to listen to his teammates was illustrated with painful regularity throughout the diaries. His command-and-control style included commanding silence and controlling the free flow of conversation. With his prevailing attitude of "himself first, the rest nowhere," Scott's overpowering self-centeredness effectively severed his few sensor tentacles at the quick.

EMPATHY

Amundsen had a very genuine personal interest in each crew member and valued his uniquely important contribution to the team's mission. As mentioned earlier, an obvious example was his appreciation and respect for Lindstrom, the cook, whose physical sustenance and sense of humor were a valuable panacea for the stresses of polar travel, especially when the ink of darkness blotted out four full months of light as they waited for summer. With his many years of active followership during prior expeditions where he was not in command, Amundsen's genuine concern for each of his companions' emotional and physical well-being was evident throughout the South Pole expedition from beginning to end, but nowhere was this more obvious than his empathic understanding of their need for camaraderie, rest, self-attainment, and fun.

While empathy is generally viewed as the ability to enter into and understand a person's feelings, leaders must include entering into and understanding their followers' *needs* every bit as much as their feelings. Very often what is needed is guidance or correction, not a feel-good moment. Leadership is about looking out for their followers' overall well-being; it is not about making them feel good—that's the easy part.

Amundsen knew that his intense empathy quickly had to

become tough empathy when appropriate, even though it may not have been what the crew member wanted to hear. Tough empathy cannot be faked over long stretches of time within the cheek-and-jowl confines of travel by sea, followed by a polar winter completely absent of sunshine, followed by confinement in a tent with others for months. It is born of dedicated mutual trust and understanding.

During this downtime, Amundsen concentrated on the improvement of individual members, knowing it would lead to team improvement and collective greatness. He told them emphatically what they needed for improvement, communicating empathetically, yet directly, on the narrow road leading to excellence. In modern times, CEO and robust board evaluations serve as effective proxies. Indeed, the ability to communicate constructively, both positively and negatively, nuances the definition of compassionate entrepreneurial leadership and is applicable not only in Amundsen's case but for leaders across every spectrum. Understanding and relating to the needs of one's followers on a personal level is an essential ingredient for leadership excellence, and often what is needed is improvement, not necessarily a pat on the back.

NOBILITY

"Noble blood is an act of fortune. Noble actions are the chief mark of greatness." —*Carlo Goldoni*

Whether chasing a gold medal in the Rio Olympics, cleansing ballast water with UV light, or being first to the South Pole for your country, Maslow's "Hierarchy of Needs" shows that mankind wants to be part of something bigger than the self. At all levels of the human strata, people do not work for bread alone; they sincerely want to make a difference in the lives of their fellow human beings.[4] It is a wise leader who can tap into this shared sense of nobility, helping others forward by creating a climate of shared mission and selflessness through one's personal example.

Both Amundsen and Scott invoked a higher cause in their polar exploration. During one of his many fundraising appeals to the public, Scott declared the goal of the expedition as follows: "The main objective of this expedition is to reach the South Pole and to secure for The British Empire the honour of this achievement."

As stated earlier, Scott's ulterior motive was to achieve military rank; he nonetheless understood the usefulness of invoking the higher cause of national pride. Although his fund-raising approach was less than entirely forthright concerning his deeper motives, Scott did possess a number of distinctly noble qualities like personal decency, moral rectitude, and a high sense of honor.

While Scott saw his quest for the pole as the next logical step in achieving his personal career goals, Amundsen saw it as the last great land journey to be completed by mankind: a full-sized canvas displaying the Norwegian flag at the South Pole planted by ten hands. In Scott's mind it was all about the painter; for Amundsen, it was always about the bigger picture. Scott sought the applause and curtain calls. Amundsen and his explorers were stagehands behind the scene.[5]

Amundsen's noble quest was inspired at the age of sixteen when Norwegian explorer Fridtjof Nansen became the first to cross the treacherous Greenland Ice Cap, a feat accomplished on skis with a remarkably small crew. Five years later when Nansen set the record for distance farthest north, 272 miles from the North Pole, Amundsen's call to explore was permanently sealed.

As Amundsen's young heart swelled with pride over Nansen's early accomplishments during the waning years of the nineteenth century, the seeds were planted for him to take part in the great sweep of Norwegian nationalism galvanized by Astrup and Nansen in their quest for sovereignty from Sweden. Amundsen saw the planting of the Norwegian flag by ten strong hands at 90° south as a way of setting Norway apart in the eyes of the world, a quest worth risking his life to accomplish.

GREAT ATTITUDE

Attitude is more important than education, money, circumstances, past failures or successes, appearance, talent, or skill. It wields enormous influence on the outcome of both leadership and followership. Unlike most leadership traits, which are developed through time and experience, attitude is a readily available renewable resource. Each person has a choice of the attitude he or she brings into every circumstance, and the 80/20 principle rules: life is 20 percent what happens and 80 percent how one reacts. With its profoundly powerful ripple effect, we alone are in charge of our attitude 24/365.

Even though technically not a leadership trait, the inestimable influence wielded by attitude is evidenced throughout the polar diaries. Like a championship team, the Norwegians shared a constructive attitude in their combined expertise, their strategy, their routine of pace, their detailed preparation, their comradeship, and their trust of one another. Their strength was in their team spirit as the Norwegians made their way to *True South*.

While not as solidly coalesced in spirit, the individual attitudes of the Englishmen were not completely dissimilar from the Norwegians'. For example, Captain Oates's serious veneer belied a perfectly splendid attitude underneath. Although he was the only crew member born into bona fide Edwardian landed gentry, he nevertheless disregarded social hierarchy and treated everyone with equal respect at all times. Known affectionately as "Soldier" or "Titus," Oates was beloved by all. Despite his wide recognition as a true war hero, he remained modest, bearing no hubris whatsoever. Absent any prideful self-centeredness, he instantly becomes every diary reader's favorite, making it hard to hold back the tears when he selflessly determines it is more important for his fellow travelers to be unfettered by his slowed pace than for him to continue the fight for his own survival. Oates's legendary chivalry, shown by giving up his life trying to save his British brothers, will be emblazoned on hearts and minds throughout generations. Year after year, Brits recount the story of brave Captain Oates gallantly dragging himself into the fangs of a raging 40-below blizzard, after quietly assuring his tent-mates, "I am just going outside and may be some time."[6]

Another of Scott's men, Marine Lieutenant Henry Bowers, was the personification of a positive attitude. He was the most indomitably rugged character on the expedition, for whom cold, fatigue, and discomfort simply did not exist. Although small in stature, Birdie Bowers was a human fireball; he had the strength of an ox, with the ability to withstand Antarctica's best weather punch, wearing a felt hat, no less! Like all great COOs, Bowers kept the trains on time with his sterling determination and can-do attitude. An intrepid fighter to the end, he was possibly the last of the five to die on their ill-fated return from the pole.[7] In his final letter of consolation to Bowers's mother as their strength faded, Scott lingered on these qualities:

> As the troubles have thickened his dauntless spirit ever shone brighter and he has remained cheerful, hopeful and indomitable to the end. The ways of Providence are inscrutable, but there must be some reason why such a young, vigorous and promising life is taken.

Dr. Edward Wilson also possessed a most upbeat attitude inspired by his deep religious beliefs. As one of the three to achieve Farthest South with Scott on the Discovery Expedition in 1903, he became one of Scott's closest friends to the extent that Scott's wife, Kathleen, developed a jealous rivalry with him. Nonetheless, Scott appointed Wilson, affectionately called "Uncle Bill," as his Chief Scientific Officer for their final Terra Nova Expedition. As they lay entombed in their tent just south of One Ton in a raging blizzard, Scott wrote to Wilson's wife, Oriana:

His eyes have a comfortable blue look of hope and his mind is peaceful with the satisfaction of his faith in regarding himself as part of the great scheme of the Almighty.

Alas, an abundance of positive attitude on the part of his crew could not save Scott's inadequate strategy and poor execution with only the help of *noblesse oblige* and education in his leadership column. Conversely, the abundance of positive attitude prevalent among the Norwegians was greatly enhanced and multiplied by Amundsen's selfless determination and tone at the top.

ESCHEWING CONCLUSION

To put Scott and Amundsen's leadership styles in purely visual terms, Amundsen's could be likened to a color wheel whose concentric circles display a range of overlapping congruent colors radiating from a midpoint, without precedence from one tone to the next; conversely, Scott's leadership would be aptly visualized as a linear value scale, with black at the top descending vertically through gradations of gray until reaching the bottom of the scale, white, or the absence of value. Like the color wheel, Amundsen's leadership style was relational and horizontal, while Scott's was hierarchical and vertical.

Simply put, Amundsen accepted all of his team as equals entitled to full respect; he likewise encouraged inclusion and camaraderie. A reading of the diaries tells that Amundsen never engaged in favoritism or played team members off of each other. Likewise, Amundsen's power was in his ability to influence, not in his positional leadership authority. He led by earning his authority, not because he had it.

Jesus Christ refused kingly title over and over again, clearing a leadership pathway to be trod over the next two thousand years, a path taken by history changers like Mahatma Gandhi, Martin Luther King, and Nelson Mandela, each a powerful leader without a leadership title. It is with a similar mindset that Amundsen included all into his polar team, while leading lightly by facilitating and encouraging heavy followership with all others.

Viewing Scott's top-down style juxtaposed alongside Amundsen's horizontal generalship, it is easy to ascertain which is the more effective approach. Scott's style also vividly illustrates the tyranny of groupthink executed by the British hierarchy. In wartime, military commands are not to be challenged due to split-second combat orders under fire.[8] Scott carried this battle-ready British naval leadership on the expedition, excluding all blue jackets at every turn, with deleterious effect. It's all he knew. As stated earlier, the crew's close quarters at Cape Evans were petitioned off for officer-scientists, leaving Edgar Evans, Crean, Lashly, Keohane, and Meares segregated in lower deck quarters. Even though ridiculously impractical, this exclusionary tactic continued into tent life even during their final trek, at Scott's insistence.

Exclusionism not only kills morale, it extinguishes every last ember of esprit de corps. On February 4, 1912, when Petty Officer Edgar Evans was already suffering from the early stages of scurvy, he fell into a crevasse up to his waist, along with Scott, as they started down Beardmore Glacier. Evans's resulting death was greatly accelerated by his palpable exclusion by all four officers, with the five of them crammed cheek-to-jowl into a tent designed for four men.

Scott was arrogant in his lack of sympathy for invalids. At the moment Evans needed comfort and encouragement, Scott ostracized him. Scott's diary entry on January 30, 1912, was a dagger of exclusion to the heart, setting the deleterious tone at the top.

> Evans had dislodged two fingernails...his hands are really bad, and to my surprise he shows signs of losing heart over it—which makes me much disappointed in him.

In this heartless atmosphere, even the normally charitable Wilson was coldly indifferent to his plight, laying Evans's deteriorating spirit off to the fact that Evans had "never been sick in his life."

Following suit with the toxic tone filtering down from the top, Captain Oates took a caustic exclusionary stand in his diary:

> It is an extraordinary thing about Evans. He has lost his guts and behaves like an old woman or worse. He is quite worn out with the work and how he is going to do the odd 400 miles we have still to

do I don't know.

Today's medical literature confirms that exclusion can leave a deeper mark than a sharp physical blow.[9] Scott had, in effect, destroyed all vestiges of camaraderie, esprit de corps, sympathy, and compassion. The heavy hand of exclusion hastened Evans's tragically solitary demise. The word "inclusionism" should be nailed as an edict on the door of the leadership world, establishing the word to its rightful place in the lexicon.

SELF REVELATION

Shedding the pretense of infallibility is a good first step in leadership. For example, the former Campbell Soup CEO, Doug Conant, was anything but bubbly like his product served hot. He was born shy, a personal trait confirmed many times by Myers-Briggs tests. He discovered the best thing to do was to simply tell everyone with whom he worked that "I'm just shy." People are not mind readers; it is important to let them know. He used his shyness to forge close relationships and build trust with employees. This is a perfect example of leadership through self-revelation. The revelation of differences and weaknesses is how the leader telegraphs humanness, and, in turn, clears a path to connect with followers on a personal level.

Amundsen acknowledged that the extraordinary skiing, dog driving, and navigational skills of his team could easily outshine his, deferring to their expertise throughout their travels, which in turn reinforced teamsmanship. On the other hand, Scott chose not to reveal anything unique about himself, much less a weakness of any sort. When this happens, followers, including Scott's men, conclude the obvious: I am not needed.

Although polar leadership was not the subject of Robert Goffee and Gareth Jones's article, "Why Should Anyone Be Lead by You?" in the *Harvard Business Review*, their writing captures the essence of Amundsen and Scott's personas.

Exposing a [leader's] weakness establishes trust and thus helps get folks on board. Indeed, if executives try to communicate that they're perfect at everything, there will be no need for anyone to help them with anything. They won't need followers. They'll signal that they can do it all themselves. Beyond creating trust and a collaborative atmosphere, communicating a weakness also builds solidarity between followers and leaders. Sharing an imperfection is so effective because it underscores a human being's authenticity.

Scott was the smartest man on the ice. His leadership flaw was flaunting it. All leaders must expose some flaws; being confident enough and humble enough to resist the charade of leadership perfection opens the door to trust and authentic relationship among coworkers.

Although some may want to assign different weight to the ten facets of leadership described in this chapter, the diaries suggest that each trait stands on its own with little in the way of priority. Remembering the mnemonic CHALLENGES[10] may be a helpful roadmap in navigating leadership challenges, great and small:

- Consistency
- Humility
- Authenticity
- Laughter
- Listening
- Empathy
- Nobility
- Great Attitude
- Ensuring Inclusion
- Self-Revelation

These ten commandments of leadership excellence apply to all leadership roles including heavy followership. As stated earlier, leadership is best learned on the job rather than in classrooms, seminars, or from books. Leadership is much more complex than management which helps explain why no definitive treatise has ever been written on leadership.[11] Even with the lessons to be learned from the polar diaries, it is important to remember that leadership is not a person. It is a process—a triangle that involves the leader, the followers, and the organization's environment and traditions.

As highly decorated retired Air Force Colonel Leon F. Ellis famously concluded, the leadership tools essential for survival while he was a POW in the Hanoi Hilton in North Vietnam are identical to those needed in boardrooms. His commendation stated that this intrepid Silver Star recipient had "resisted [the enemy's] demands by calling upon his deepest inner strengths." Similarly, in surveying the topic of leadership through the template of the polar explorers, one can see that this is always the permanent home where true leadership dwells: deep within. Amundsen's compassionate entrepreneurial leadership is its personification.

It is not an oversimplification to suggest that within the fountainhead of compassionate entrepreneurial leadership flow the necessary tools for solving many of mankind's major challenges looming on the horizon from now until Kingdom Come.

Notes

1. *The Last Place on Earth*, Roland Huntford, Chapter 11, p. 151.
2. David Brooks reiterated this theme in his *New York Times* article, "Temerity at the Top," September 21, 2012: "Today grandiosity is out of style. We've been through a financial crisis fueled by people who got too big for their britches."
3. Dr. Lane Anderson.
4. New research conducted by Stanford professor Chip Heath while a professor at Duke University's Fuqua School of Business concluded that Maslow failed to put enough emphasis on the psychological needs, such as self-fulfillment and learning new skills. J. Phillips L. Johnston, *Biscuitville: The Secret Recipe for Building a Sustainable Competitive Advantage* (Easton Studio Press, 2009).
5. In the journal *In Character*, *Washington Post* theater critic Peter J. Marks discusses the ethos of stagehands who are motivated by communal work, not applause. Communal work, esprit de corps, and contribution to the whole production are infinitely more important than applause in the limelight.
6. Even though recorded by Scott, there is little doubt that Oates uttered these now-famous parting words. The unassuming succinctness is vintage Oates. Scott would have categorically honored a fellow officer's dying declaration, and if he had indeed chosen to tamper with his word choice, he would have embellished it with a flourish of eloquence.
7. Lieutenant Henry Robertson Bowers died on March 29, 1912, at the age of twenty-nine. Each member in the party got equal rations. Bowers's five-foot-four-inch height was a distinct advantage.
8. Dr. Lane Anderson.
9. Loneliness is a risk factor for functional decline and early death in adults over age sixty, according to a University of California, San Francisco study by Dr. Carla Perissinotto, MD, MHS published in the

Achieves of Internal Medicine July 2012. More than 43 percent of the 1,604 participants reported that they often felt left out or isolated or lacked companionship. In the six-year follow-up period, more than half of the self-identified lonely people had a 45 percent greater risk of dying earlier than older adults who felt more connected to others. This is further evidence of the debilitating effect of Evans's ostracism.

10. The mnemonic CHALLENGES telegraphs the pathway to compassionate entrepreneurial leadership.

11. Even Jim Collins's book, *Good to Great*, is somewhat flawed in retrospect. The definition of successful performance for these eleven companies depends crucially on the period considered. Likewise, in her recent book, *The End of Leadership*, Barbara Kellerman casts a critical eye on institutions claiming to effectively develop and teach leaders. Dr. Kellerman is the James MacGregor Burns Lecturer in Public Leadership at Harvard University's John F. Kennedy School of Government and is an international authority on the subject of followership.

CHAPTER 12.

MORALITY

America is great because America is good, and if America ever ceases to be good, America ceases to be great.
–ALEXIS DE TOCQUEVILLE

Morality is not a leadership trait. It is much bigger. Morality is a fundamental part of the leadership value system; it is so fundamental, in fact, that we fully expect it at all times and only think about it when we are shocked by a discovery of its absence within an individual leader or institution. To state the obvious, a lack of moral integrity greatly diminishes the respect and trust required for leadership. Who would knowingly want to follow the leadership of a felon, blatant liar, or serial adulterer?

Oddly enough, it is on the subject of morality that the polar explorers provide counterevidence to the importance of leadership markers. It is an anomaly that Amundsen's chronic habits of adultery and immoderate drinking did not rise to the level of concern among his followers. In the biographical film *Frozen Heart* we learn of Amundsen's string of dysfunctional relationships with the opposite sex, starting with his own mother. His adult relationships were always with beautiful women who were married to prominent men. In his own words, Amundsen showed his hand by clearly establishing his Viking view of the other sex: "The god of happiness is a woman. If you want her, you have to grab her and carry her off."

Conversely, there is every indication that Scott was an absolute gentleman, completely faithful to his unfaithful wife. Moreover, Scott's overall morality was water-tight.

Even though Amundsen was not a boozer, he, like the acclaimed British explorer Earnest Shackleton popped the cork with gusto and was a highly advanced adulterer. Nonetheless, like Shackleton, Amundsen was adored by his men, possibly because of their shared isolation on the extremely perilous battlefield of polar exploration. In Shackleton's very blunt words: "Not a life lost, and we have been through hell."

Similarly, Amundsen never suffered the loss of one of his men on either the expedition to the Northwest Passage or the South Pole.[1]

The evidence from the diaries that intemperance and adultery is to be overlooked in leadership is false teaching. Under no circumstances should it be concluded that debauchery and lasciviousness could ever be viewed as an acceptable part of the leadership equation.

What is Character?

Character is doing the right thing at the right time for the right reasons. Leadership is character in action. We manage things and lead people.

Character cannot be taught from a book but only by the personal example of significant positive role models. The opposite of character results when negative role models are emulated because striving in a positive direction is perceived to be too difficult, too dull, or too slow in fulfilling one's needs or life ambitions.

Character is the opposite of self-centeredness. Compassion, empathy, and charity are the emotional qualities of character and provide purpose to outward actions.

To a person with character, obstacles and difficulties in life are perceived as challenges to be overcome with confidence, optimism, and persistence. Overcoming adversity is the chief means through which character is developed. The result is always increased self-esteem, which is essential if one is to have the character to serve others.

Courage and good judgment are also essential components of

character. To stand up for one's ideals, no matter how difficult the circumstances, requires fortitude based on a core set of positive values. The judgment to assess and act in difficult and "gray" areas in life situations requires a decisiveness which can only come from character continuously strengthened by time and experience.

—Dr. Lane S. Anderson, III, Ed.D.

The importance of moral character, especially in leadership, cannot be overstated. A healthy society is dependent on it.

Notes

1. While at the helm as first mate on the Belgica Antarctic Expedition 1897–1899, Wiencke, a Norwegian seaman, was cast into the angry sea during a storm off South Shetland Islands and died. Amundsen unfortunately assumed the blame and grieved forever.

CHAPTER 13.

A CLOSING WORD ON FOLLOWERSHIP

What have we gleaned from these two polar opposite explorers to advance our understanding of leadership for the betterment of today's world? Simply put, leadership can be learned. As evidenced by the new growth industry of leadership education, the principles of leadership can be taught; however, leadership is *learned* in the laboratory of life. Not only can it be learned in one's daily life, but counter-intuitively it is learned from the bottom up. By simple math, most leadership lessons are learned in the heavy followership moment because the majority of our time is spent following. Even the CEO is a "direct report." In our younger years, almost all of our leadership bearings are established in day-to-day heavy followership. Principles and concepts can be learned from the pages of a textbook, but leadership is learned over the long term, in the quotidian lessons gathered in the classroom of everyday life. Contrary to MBA thinking, leadership-learning experiences often occur in the context of daily heavy followership when working in a group.

Followership is where the empathy of leadership originates—one learns empathetic leadership having first been a follower. As a corollary, we know that all great leaders were first great followers, or in Aristotle's insightful words, "He who never learned to obey cannot be a good leader."

It is important to bear in mind the obvious truth that leaders

LIGHT LEADERSHIP/HEAVY FOLLOWERSHIP CONTINUUM

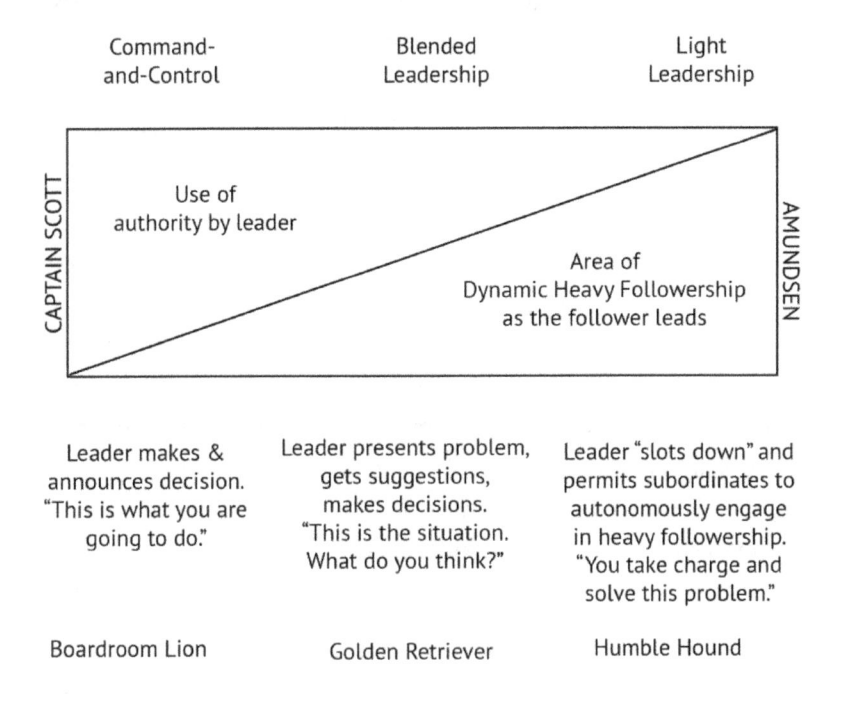

	Command-and-Control	Blended Leadership	Light Leadership
	Use of authority by leader		
			Area of Dynamic Heavy Followership as the follower leads
	Leader makes & announces decision. "This is what you are going to do."	Leader presents problem, gets suggestions, makes decisions. "This is the situation. What do you think?"	Leader "slots down" and permits subordinates to autonomously engage in heavy followership. "You take charge and solve this problem."
	Boardroom Lion	Golden Retriever	Humble Hound

Left axis: CAPTAIN SCOTT. Right axis: AMUNDSEN.

cannot lead if they do not have followers. While many erroneously believe having followers requires charisma, we know that charisma can be destructive. Stalin, Mao, Pol Pot, and even Bernie Ebbers and Jeffrey Skilling all reveal the dark underbelly of this quality; all of these leaders were highly charismatic by many accounts, yet they prove that far from being a necessity, an abundance of charisma can lead to personal doom, not only for the charismatic leader, but more importantly, the masses of unsuspecting followers.[1]

On the other hand, page after page of the polar diaries show that one cannot be an effective leader without authenticity, empathy, inclusion, and humility in caring for one's followers. Wise leaders know the power of followership and how to nurture it on a day-to-day basis:

- "The longer I study effective leaders, the more I am convinced of the under-appreciated importance of effective followers." This comment by leadership guru Warren Bennis argues that "followership" has been neglected in comparison to leadership, that leadership and followership are not contraries but aspects of the same thing. The future trend is towards light leadership and heavy followership.

- An effective, committed follower is able to lead upward; in other words, followership often includes leading. These heavy followers become informal leaders by active engagement, taking responsibility for their area of expertise within the bigger picture. Olav Bjaaland, Olympic ski expert, Helmer Hanssen, expert surveyor, Sverre Hassel, expert dog driver, and Oscar Wisting, dog expert and self-trained veterinarian, each with their superior know-how, exercised heavy followership almost daily with Amundsen's active encouragement.

- This same followership model can be found at most professional service firms, especially larger law offices and medical practices where each professional, by necessity, moves fluidly from leader to follower depending on their respective specializations. In other environments, heavy followership or light leadership can depend far more on attitude than on knowledge and experience. This means that even traditional manufacturing enterprises can adopt the concept of heavy followership; the management simply needs to empower the skilled employees by encouraging greater participation and input.

- Even though those who know what to do will always be in charge of and lead those who know how to do a task, the ability of the leader to delegate to followers with superior skills he or she trusts and respects is essential in complex operations.[2]

- Ultimately there is little difference between the skill sets of following and leading because heavy followers and light leaders share the same leadership traits of listening well, empathizing with others' points of view, and showing respect for those they are leading or following. In fact, all ten leadership qualities captured in our CHALLENGES mnemonic apply to both light leadership and those in heavy followership!

- In The Art of Followership, Ronald E. Riggio, Ira Chaleff, and Jean Lipman-Blumen point out: "Following and leading are not roles or even mindsets but internal activities within the same person who can switch from leading to following and back again in an instant. In today's less-hierarchical, knowledge-based organizations, good followership may be even more important to organizational success than good leadership."

- It should be emphasized that that heavy followership is especially critical in today's technology start-ups, which have the combination of technical brainiacs and seasoned business professionals collaborating in an environment of rapid change and substantial ambiguity, amid a steady stream (or overflow) of new information emanating from the bottom up, all with very little infrastructure in place.

POLAR FOLLOWERSHIP

The desire to be needed is one of life's most fundamental callings.

Scott's crew members recognized that they were not particularly needed because Scott's heavy-handed attitude clearly telegraphed this message to remind them on a daily basis. Scott's example evidences the stormy waters that emerge in the wake of rigid top-down leadership, with its treacherous results clearly manifested throughout his failed journey. As established earlier, while Scott's charisma was undeniable his leadership style crippled all chances of the kind of followership, esprit de corps, and

Staking True South: Absent an adequate horizon that day, a tray of mercury on a stand is used as an artificial horizon in order for the sextant to reconfirm the exact location of the Pole.

collective excellence that wins the race.

One can easily observe the reverse approach by taking a look at Scott's polar opposite, Amundsen, who possessed all the charisma of a withered fig tree. Charisma's insignificance in leadership is clearly illustrated throughout the diaries, but especially in Amundsen's contrasting style shown in his skillful articulation of the essential value of light leadership and heavy followership.

The combination of both light leadership and heavy followership is the very essence of teamwork.

Upon reaching the South Pole on December 14, 1911, the Norwegians spent a full three days surveying at Polheim, headed by crew member Helmer Hanssen. The first men to take the prize wanted to make absolutely certain they precisely marked the geographic pole because they were aware of the amateur-hour antics of both false claimers of the North Pole.

Skiers fanned out in each direction to crisscross the plateau, planting markers using their navigational instruments to take twenty-four sextant readings. Reading the diary accounts of their days at Polheim provides especially rich data displaying the effectiveness and efficiency of heavy followership, with Hanssen and then Bjaaland moving in and out of leadership periods encouraged by Amundsen as he slotted down. Their work attitude and camaraderie also showed that the followers had established well-hewn standards of behavior. In sports parlance this is known as putting the ball where you know your teammate is going to be.

Their skillful collaboration and festive mood stretched unabated throughout these three days. On December 17, 1911, the last evening at the pole, the normally taciturn Olav Bjaaland amazed the crew with a moving impromptu speech about how they had, indeed, accomplished the feat explorers had dreamed of for centuries. At the end of his felicitous address, he surprised his friends by pulling out the case of fine cigars he had secretly carried throughout their treacherous journey. As they reveled in their shared success into the night, surely they were on the top of the world at the bottom of the world celebrating under the canopy of polar twilight, while the cold Antarctic wind replied by whisking the sounds of their exultation across the miles and miles of frozen emptiness.

At the end of the long day, with his characteristic humility and unsentimental succinctness, Amundsen, after chronicling Bjaaland's remarks, recorded a six-word testament to the shared accomplishment of these five triumphant polar leaders and followers: "What do you say to that?"

Notes

1. Peter Drucker, an expert on leadership, in his last interview when he was ninety-five, told Rich Karlgaard and Dr. Rick Warren about the danger of charisma:

   > The most charismatic leaders of the last century were called Hitler, Stalin, Mao and Mussolini. They were mis-leaders! Charismatic leadership by itself certainly is greatly overstated. Look, one of the most effective American presidents of the last 100 years was Harry Truman. He didn't have an ounce of charisma. Truman was as bland as a dead mackerel. Everybody who worked for him worshipped him because he was absolutely trustworthy. If Truman said no, it was no, and if he said yes, it was yes. And he didn't say no to one person and yes to the next one on the same issue. The other effective president of the last 100 years was Ronald Reagan. His great strength was not charisma, as is commonly thought, but that he knew exactly what he could do and what he could not do.

2. Dr. Lane Anderson.

CHAPTER 14.

EPILOGUE: AMUNDSEN'S TARNISHED GOLD IN RETIREMENT

A leader with Amundsen's accomplishments surely earned the reward of a quiet retirement: the sheer wonderment of hearing silence between notes struck in the golden years.

Alas, the master of compassionate entrepreneurial leadership instead went on to fail Retirement 101. Like many famous athletes, corporate chieftains, politicians, theologians, and even great leaders like Napoleon, Amundsen overstayed his welcome on the world stage.

Consider the fate of Napoleon, who incidentally was Captain Oates's hero to the extent that his portrait was hauled to Antarctica and mounted in the officers' dining area at Cape Evans. As historian Paul Johnson wrote about Nappy:

> Know yourself, know your people, know your job (mission). Key ingredients. The lesson from his life is clear: The important thing about success is knowing when to stop. Had Napoleon stopped after his victory over the Russians and Austrians at Austerlitz, he'd have enjoyed a long and honorable retirement and gone down in history as a man of moderation whose brilliance never obscured his judgment. As it was, he went from victories to near defeats to outright defeat and humiliating exile on a rock in the Atlantic. The number of successful businessmen who haven't learned this lesson is legion—and growing all the time.

George Washington was one of the very few leaders wise enough to exit the career stage right on cue. After liberating the thirteen colonies, Washington quietly retired to his farm in Virginia. Only after being called by the unanimous voice of the people did he enter politics. Even then, he tried to stay at Mt. Vernon.

As a leader, Amundsen towered above his rivals with his elegant approach to strategy. The tarnishing of one's golden years in retirement is not about leadership; it is about the difficulty of looking inward to know the right time to exit gracefully, before the jerk of the sheep hook announces the passing of one's prime.

Amundsen's conquest of the South Pole immortalized him on the world stage. Equal to that feat, he was also the first man—after many attempts over the 382 years prior, beginning with Giovanni Verrazano—to conquer the Northwest Passage.

To his credit, Amundsen's way of speaking and writing was to simply report the facts, instead of dramatizing or dwelling on his accomplishments. However, the downside of his personal humility is that when telling of his travels, his writing was dry, and his lectures were even dryer. Then to further exacerbate his loss of public appeal, by the age of only forty-one, the elements had reduced his face into gritty creases of toughened leather; he looked more like an octogenarian than a middle-aged man. Unable to keep the public excited, he made very little money with the book he wrote, and before long requests for speaking engagements dried up completely. His post-1912 life was an arid plateau—dry words, dry speeches, dry face, and dry pockets.

On the other hand, Scott's legacy expanded to be larger than life in his death. Amid the throes of his tragic death, his legacy was being birthed. His journals expressed the romantic view of duty, struggle, sacrifice, and incredible bravery in facing death. His wife connived to remove every diary entry impugning his leadership.[1] This maneuver coupled with Scott's considerable writing skills vaulted Scott's last days, so poignantly described in his diaries, into a message of hope and inspiration, a lesson on enduring hardship and suffering in the British tradition. Because of his team's perseverance in collecting thirty pounds of geological specimens right up to the end (even after it became apparent that their very lives were in severe jeopardy), their narrative transformed into a demonstration of supreme self-sacrifice. Scott's pluck, manhood, and strength, and Oates's extreme courage in the face of death, were repeatedly recounted by drill instructors training Tommies for the horrors of the guns of August and beyond.

It was as though Scott, an upper-class Edwardian gentleman, had plucked sainthood out of the jaws of death itself right at the same moment that Amundsen faded into the haze, a forgotten hero on a distant horizon. Even though Amundsen's grief over Scott was sincere, being relegated to the trash bin of has-beens hurt him deeply. He dedicated his remaining years attempting to recapture the glory Scott's death had stolen from him.

Aviation became his new world to conquer. Amundsen began flying lessons two years after his return from the pole in 1914, and was the first to receive a civilian pilot's certificate in Norway. In the 1920s, searching for new challenges, Amundsen made several unsuccessful attempts to fly over the North Pole. His early flights failed to set new records, and the press criticized him severely. The cost of aviation coupled with diminishing income from book royalties and lecture fees caused a falling-out with his brother Leon, his business manager. As daring as his new flying adventures were, without the needed financial clout, Amundsen had to surrender control to others; he was no longer the commander and ultimately participated more as a passenger. Financially strapped, he became increasingly embittered, frequently lashing out at old allies. Hounded by a legion of unsympathetic creditors, his financial health, always precarious, was now in a state of collapse. Creditors are unimpressed by fame; Amundsen filed for bankruptcy in 1924.

Still unable to exit the center stage limelight of his heroic feats won at the South Pole and Northwest Passage, Amundsen joined Lincoln Ellsworth, a New Yorker who turned the expending of inherited Wall Street wealth into an art form. A quintessential

Roaring Twenties dandy, Ellsworth could have stepped out of an F. Scott Fitzgerald novel. During another ill-planned venture to fly over the North Pole, the two crashed on the way, yet nevertheless managed to set a record for Farthest North. Amundsen regained some of his lost popularity as their heroic escape from death was recorded in the press as a triumph of sorts.

In 1926, Amundsen and young Ellsworth embarked on yet another attempt to fly over the North Pole, this time in a dirigible, *The Norge*. Just before their dirigible venture, Richard E. Byrd claimed himself to be the first to fly an airplane *to* the North Pole. Nevertheless *The Norge*, which was designed and piloted by Italian Umberto Nobile, became the first to fly *across* the North Pole. The aftermath of *The Norge* excursion was miserable. A feud between Amundsen and Nobile over who deserved the most credit was waged in full view of the world press, with Amundsen getting the worst of the coverage. This unfortunate conflict, combined with the constant pursuit by his creditors, exacerbated Amundsen's bitter state tremendously.

Amundsen retired again in 1926. Then two years later, when Umberto Nobile disappeared in the airship *Italia* on a flight to the North Pole, Amundsen came out of retirement declaring it his duty to save a fellow explorer, even though his deep hatred of Nobile had been well publicized. When the Italian dictator Benito Mussolini, who was still quite exercised over their earlier feud, exerted pressure from Italy, Norway quietly dropped Amundsen from their offer to form a rescue party.

Even with the rejection of his motherland, Amundsen joined a private rescue attempt with Leif Dietrichson and Captain René Guilbaud flying a French-manufactured Latham 47 fitted with floats. There were numerous other rescue attempts by twenty aircraft and a fleet of ships from Sweden, France, Finland, and Italy at the same time. After Amundsen and his two flying mates had been flying for three days with very little sleep, at four o'clock on June 18, 1928, the would-be rescuers taxied for takeoff from Tromso, north of Spitsbergen, headed for the arctic. Lumbering into thick banks of summer fog dangerously impeding visibility, the heavily laden plane struggled mightily as it became airborne. Soon thereafter, radio contact went silent.

Amundsen's last quest belies his well-deserved reputation for meticulous preparation and careful weighing of risks and rewards. Under modern scrutiny, the combination of risks taken in his final journey was quite high. This devil-may-care behavior is completely out of character with the months of fastidious preparation preceding the polar journey, which included laying down depots much farther south than Scott with over three times the food and paraffin, reducing the weight of sledges 50 percent, using Netsilik Eskimo loose reindeer skin clothing for warmth and ventilation, reducing the width and increasing the length of the skis, redesigning a five-man tent with the ease of one pole set-up and waterproof floor covering, and cutting side slits in goggles to minimize snow blindness. Amundsen considered every detail with focused seriousness in response to his profound respect for the ice he was to confront. Additionally, Amundsen fully identified with the historian who said, "In Norway there is very little tolerance for failure in expeditions. You go and you come back whole."

Curiously, Amundsen was poised to get married later that year to Bess Magids, a thirty-one-year-old Alaskan who had just finalized her divorce from the proprietor of a chain of trading stations because of her lengthy affair with Amundsen. Adultery was nothing new with Amundsen, whose predilection for beautiful married women led him into earlier affairs with Sigrid Castberg, the wife of a well-known Norwegian lawyer, and Kristine Bennett, the wife of a successful British landed aristocrat, two of his more notable conquests—maybe not a girl in every port, but certainly a lady friend in several countries. His uncharacteristic determination to ignore the obvious risks of his ill-planned flight suggests the possibility that this solitary man was escaping the grips of his impending commitment. And escape, he did; the only evidence of his tragic end was a petrol tank, which had been screwed off and used as an improvised life raft. Umberto Nobile was rescued by another party. Amundsen died at sea at the age of fifty-six; his remains rest on its deep dark floor, unfound.

On a final note, like his famous ancestors who discovered America in 1001, the last Viking surely carried out a death wish for a sea grave. In the early days, the Vikings were known for burial customs that involved great ceremony. Traditionally, the corpses of rich Viking men and as many as three living wives and all living slaves were buried in a ship grave, along with their jewelry, beds, weapons, and live dogs. At times, the dead Viking's ship was torched as it was pushed out to sea.

It is somehow fitting that the greatest polar explorer and Viking to the core was quietly laid to rest below the depths of the Arctic Ocean as the curtain call for his final adventure. His famously pithy self-deprecating estimation of his near-death experience on an early skiing expedition with his brother Leon brings a heart-wrenching sense of irony to his tragic demise: "Adventure is just bad planning."

Notes

1. There were over seventy material excisions, including the humiliation of Norwegian team member and ski expert, Tryggve Gran.

THE CAST

FRAM EXPEDITION

Norwegian Explorers Who Reached the South Pole First with Amundsen:

OLAV O. BJAALAND (1873–1961) was a Norwegian ski champion who viewed the quest for the pole as a cross-country race, only on a much larger scale. In preparation for the journey, he redesigned skis not to warp, designed custom bindings, and took an incredible fifty pounds of weight off the heavier sledges while cutting the total weight of the lighter ones by half. Bjaaland also became the team's unofficial photographer when he captured their historic arrival at the South Pole by taking the only two pictures of the entire Fram Expedition using his personal Kodak. Always possessing an insightful way with words, he kept an extensive diary observing everything from conversations to details about their food to the panoramic wonders surrounding them—describing, for instance, their first sighting of the ice barrier:

> At long last, the ice barrier hove into sight today. It is a strange feeling that grips one as the sight now reveals itself. The sea is still as a pool, and before one stands this Great Wall of China and glitters.

Far off, it is like a photograph that has just been developed on the plate.

Bjaaland was a consummate team player; while he understood that Amundsen was first among equals, he frequently and effectively stepped into leadership with quiet finesse whenever his expertise was needed. Upon their safe return to Norway, Amundsen was the first to help Bjaaland finance his new ski-manufacturing company.

HELMER J. HANSSEN (1870–1956) sailed with Amundsen as second mate on the *Gjoa*, which was the first Arctic expedition to successfully navigate the Northwest Passage. Later, on the Fram Expedition, he was in charge of navigation and also provided invaluable expertise as a dog driver. His year with the Inuit Eskimos in Northern Canada prepared him well for travelling the frigid polar extremes. Taking the lead during the three days they spent triple-checking the exact geographic South Pole, he demonstrated that leadership is often a shared process within a cohesive team. Hanssen later joined Amundsen a third time on the Maud Expedition.

SVERRE H. HASSEL (1876–1928) was an experienced dog driver trained on a prior polar expedition by the master, Otto Sverdrup, who perfected the use of huskies as draft animals by incorporating insights gained from the Inuits. Even though Hassel privately noted in his diary that Amundsen could sometimes be hard to work with, he still greatly admired his leadership, writing that "Captain Amundsen is a wonderful man. We could never have accomplished the journey without him." Amundsen's honest admission of his occasional tendency to be cantankerous strengthened their bonds of friendship. Hassel stayed in touch with Amundsen throughout his life, and to Amundsen's great sadness, died while visiting Amundsen's home in Uranienborg.

OSCAR WISTING (1871–1936) was one of Amundsen's longest-serving, most trusted compatriots; he travelled with him to both the North and South Pole. A young gunner in the Norwegian Navy, he was selected by Amundsen for the Fram Expedition because of his steady demeanor and his proven ability to withstand hard work in frigid weather. In their later attempt to reach the North Pole, Wisting assumed command of the Maud Expedition when Amundsen left in 1922, and rejoined Amundsen in 1926 aboard the airship *Norge* to be the first to cross the North Pole by dirigible. In 1936, on a sentimental visit to the *Fram*, which was then undergoing restoration in Norway, he quietly passed away while lying in his old bunk, suffering a heart attack at the age of 65.

Other Fram Expedition Members:

H. FREDRIK GJERTSEN (1885–1958) was a Lieutenant in the Norwegian Navy and an officer on the *Fram*.

F. HJALMAR JOHANSEN (1867–1913) was a highly experienced polar trekker who accompanied Nansen aboard the *Fram* from 1893 to 1895. Additionally, he was the great explorer's only companion on his ski trip to Franz Josef Land in 1895. Later, Nansen insisted that Amundsen include Johansen on his South Pole expedition, but Amundsen soon dismissed Johansen for fiercely lambasting his leadership in front of the other men, following their premature departure for the pole. Depressed, penniless, and suffering from alcoholism, he committed suicide after his return to Norway in January of 1913.

ADOLPH H. LINDSTROM (1866–1939) accompanied Amundsen on both the *Gjoa* and the *Fram* as cook; additionally, Lindstrom maintained the home base at Framheim while the polar and eastern parties were away exploring. He and Amundsen elevated humor to a leadership art form with their good-natured bantering.

THORVALD NILSEN (1881–1940) was a lieutenant in the Norwegian Navy and captain of the *Fram*. He commanded the ship during the oceanographic survey of the South Atlantic, which took place while Amundsen and his team were making their journey to the pole.

KRISTIAN PRESTRUD (1881–1927) was a lieutenant in the Norwegian Navy who joined the shore party at the Bay of Whales. He nearly froze to death during Amundsen's quickly aborted, ill-timed start to the South Pole in September of 1911, but he was saved by Hjalmar Johansen. Prestrud later led the eastern party to explore uncharted King Edward VII Land accompanied by Johansen, who had been demoted for insubordination.

JORGEN STUBBERUD (1883–1980) was a carpenter from Oslo who constructed the home base "observation hut" that became Framheim. He also participated in the eastern party.

TERRA NOVA EXPEDITION

The Final Party That Accompanied Scott to the Pole:

HENRY R. BOWERS ("Birdie;" 1883–1912) was a lieutenant in the Royal Indian Marines with no prior polar experience. Even so, his efficient organization, personal humility, cheerful outlook, and astonishing constitution made him an invaluable team player and easily the most respected on the Terra Nova Expedition. Despite being the smallest crew member, Bowers was equal in strength to both Taff Evans and Robert Scott, with their much larger builds; Scott's diary fairly gushed with acclaim for him. In Bowers's final letter to his mother, he reassuringly told her, "You will know that for me the end was peaceful as it is only sleep in the cold."

EDGAR EVANS ("Taff;" 1876–1912) was a career petty officer in the Royal Navy (hence "P.O. Evans" in the diaries). Having been a crew member on both of Scott's expeditions, he was a favorite of Scott's, mainly because of his physical strength and mechanical ability needed to maintain equipment. When Taff became severely disabled early on the return trip from the pole, the other four team members who were officers ostracized him. He died February 17, 1912.

LAWRENCE E. G. OATES ("Titus," "Soldier;" 1880–1912) was captain of the 6th (Inniskilling) Dragoons in the British cavalry where he earned the sobriquet "No Surrender" after being wounded during an ambush in the Second Boer War. Because of his cavalry experience, he was put in charge of the ponies during the Terra Nova Expedition. After his feet developed severe, disabling frostbite, Oates heroically sacrificed himself on his thirty-second birthday so as not to impede the others. In league with General Robert E. Lee, Oates's legendary chivalry is immortalized in Charles Dollman's painting, *A Very Gallant Gentleman.* One cannot read the polar diaries without being awed by his abject humility, likability, and brave heart. Out of line with Oates's highborn place within the British upper crust and landed gentry, his mother often referred to Robert Scott as her son's "murderer" with uncharacteristic candor.

EDWARD A. WILSON ("Uncle Bill;" 1872–1912) was a physician, painter, naturalist, and Scott's closest confidant. After reading Natural Sciences at Gonville and Caius College, Cambridge, he moved to London to study medicine. Wilson was first assigned to Scott's *Discovery* as surgeon and naturalist and then rejoined him on the *Terra Nova*, where he earned universal admiration for his intelligence and selflessness. His moral leadership lent gravitas to the belief in the practice of man-hauling, thus helping to bring Markham and Scott's fateful strategy full pivot. Although less well known than Ponting's photographs, Wilson's beautiful sketches and watercolors uniquely capture the sublime mystery of Antarctica. A deeply religious man, his last letter to his wife, Oriana, concluded, "Your little testament and prayer book will be in my hand or in my breast pocket when the end comes. All is well...." Despite his many amiable qualities, Dr. Wilson must still be held accountable for his failure to sufficiently warn Scott that Oates's reemerging war wounds and Taff's festering cut should have precluded their selection for the last treacherous leg to the pole.

Other Notable Participants in the British Southern Journey 1911–1912:

EDWARD L. ATKINSON ("Atch;" 1881–1929) was a Royal Navy surgeon and trained parasitologist. Atkinson was a member of the first support party that accompanied Scott onto the Polar Plateau. He was put in command at Cape Evans after Lieutenant Teddy Evans departed for England in March 1912. With Lieutenant Victor Campbell trapped on Inexpressible Island, he ended up leading the relief party that found Scott's last camp.

VICTOR L. A. CAMPBELL ("The Wicked Mate;" 1875–1956) was a Royal Navy lieutenant who was appointed to lead the eastern party to King Edward VII Land, which was then completely unexplored. Finding the *Fram* uncomfortably close to his target, he switched to South Victoria Land and his expedition became the northern party. Because of difficulties with the pack ice, his team was not relieved by ship and had to spend the winter of 1912 with inadequate supplies and shelter.

APSLEY G. B. CHERRY-GARRARD ("Cherry;" 1886–1959) was twenty-four years old when he was hired as assistant biologist on the Terra Nova Expedition, making him the second youngest of the crew. When Scott's return from the pole was overdue, Cherry was part of the small party dispatched to One Ton Camp; filled with regret for not going farther, he was haunted for years by severe self-reproach for choosing to turn back, leaving Scott, Wilson, and Bowers to die. After returning from Antarctica, Cherry developed clinical depression (today's post-traumatic stress disorder) as well as irritable bowel syndrome. In 1922, he wrote *The Worst Journey in the World* about his grueling austral winter journey to Cape Crozier, the penguin breeding ground on the eastern edge of Ross Island, at the urging of his close friend and wealthy neighbor, George Bernard Shaw. In addition to being an excellent adventure story, it is a complex, dark meditation on the significance of exploration. Writing helped his PTSD, but he stayed bedridden most of his life. In 1939, Cherry unexpectedly married Angela Turner, thirty years his junior, at the outbreak of the Second World War. They chose not to have children for fear of passing down his mental health problems. He enjoyed a relatively content domestic life, but never escaped the burden of his polar regrets.

THOMAS CREAN (1876–1938) was a petty officer in the Royal Navy. He received the prestigious Albert Medal for his incredible eighteen-hour solo march to Hut Point to bring back help for the gravely ill Lieutenant Teddy Evans on their return from the Polar Plateau. A true team player, he was a polar explorer extraordinaire with superlative ability and determination. One of the great mysteries of Scott's polar expedition is that he did not include Crean to make the final trek to the pole, choosing far less physically capable travelers instead. Later Crean served on the Endurance Expedition and made the heroic crossing of South Georgia with Shackleton and Worsley in May of 1916, which resulted in the eventual rescue of the men marooned on Elephant Island.

BERNARD C. DAY ("Rivets;" 1884–1965) was a young engineer who drove the first car in Antarctica while on Shackleton's Nimrod Expedition. Several years later, he was placed in charge of the motor sledges on the Terry Nova Expedition but failed to prepare properly by putting them through their paces in Europe before heading south. After the ensuing breakdown of all the sledges in Antarctica, he man-hauled with the others on Scott's southern journey almost to the Transantarctic Mountains. Following his return from Antarctica, Day served in the First World

War and later worked as an engineer in Australia, where he eventually died in a car accident.

FRANK DEBENHAM ("Deb;" 1883–1965) was an Australian geologist who served on the scientific staff of the Terra Nova Expedition. Later, he was named the first director of the Scott Polar Research Institute in Cambridge, UK.

EDWARD R. G. R. EVANS ("Teddy;" 1880–1957) was a Royal Navy officer bearing a five-letter monogram: Edward Ratcliffe Garth Russell Evans. He was educated at Merchant Taylor's and on board HMS *Worcester,* before becoming an officer in 1896. After serving on the *Morning*'s relief of the *Discovery* from 1902 to 1903, Evans planned his own Welsh Antarctic expedition, but at Markham's insistence, he agreed to serve as Scott's second in command instead. Scott, the martinet, made no secret of his animosity toward Evans; his contempt drove him to take Evans's name in vain in his diaries and eventually thwart his command by curtailing his duties. Undaunted by Scott's plan to break and eliminate him, Evans went on to achieve international fame during the First World War as commander of the destroyer HMS *Broke*—which, alongside only one other British ship, attacked six German destroyers intent on bombarding Dover in 1917. After some bloody hand-to-hand fighting, three of the German destroyers were disabled, three retreated, and over one hundred prisoners were taken. Evans was reported to have shouted, "Remember the *Lusitania*!" to the Germans clamoring to be rescued. He retired as Admiral Lord Mountevans, becoming a Labour peer, Baron Mountevans.

DIMITRI GEROFF (1888–1932) was a dog driver brought from Siberia by Cecil Meares. He went as far as the base of the Beardmore Glacier with the southern party and later accompanied Cherry-Garrard in March of 1912 to One Ton Depot, failing to find Scott's party.

TRYGGVE GRAN ("Trigger;" 1889–1980) was a ski expert on the Terra Nova Expedition. Gran had begun preparations for his own polar journey when the great Norwegian explorer Fridtjof Nansen recommended him to Scott. Although Scott's opinion of the Norwegian later improved, numerous early criticisms of Gran were removed from the journal published by Kathleen Bruce Scott. He was a member of the relief party that found Scott's final camp in November of 1912, and sixteen years later played a key role in the search for Amundsen, who had himself been lost during the search for Umberto Nobile's ill-fated North Pole airship expedition. In the interim, Gran became a fighter pilot during the First World War and downed seventeen German planes as a member of the Royal Flying Corps. He was the youngest officer among the *Terra Nova*'s shore party and the last to die.

PATRICK KEOHANE ("Patsy;" 1879–1950) was a petty officer who served with Teddy Evans on HMS *Talbot* and was a member of the first support party. He participated in the search that found Scott's last camp.

WILLIAM LASHLY (Also spelled Lashley; 1867–1940) was chief stoker in the Royal Navy. His modesty and loyalty elevated him to become the "Wilson of the lower deck." Earning a splendid reputation for dependability on the earlier Discovery Expedition, he accompanied Scott onto the Polar Plateau, returning in early January of 1912 with Teddy Evans and Crean. During their return trip, he stayed with Evans, who was near death with scurvy, while Crean went for help; if Crean hadn't reached Hut Point, all in the party would have died. Both he and Crean received the Albert Medal for heroism.

CECIL H. MEARES ("Mother;" 1877–1937) was an adventurer and probably a British spy; he was also an expert dog handler. He traveled to Siberia to secure the dogs and ponies for the Terra Nova Expedition and transported them to New Zealand.

He accompanied Scott as far as the base of the Beardmore Glacier and then returned to Cape Evans.

HERBERT G. PONTING ("Ponco;" 1870–1935) was the expedition's official photographer who documented many aspects of life in and around Cape with still photos and movie film. The most famous photographic images of the heroic age were captured by Ponco's cameras.

RAYMOND EDWARD PRIESTLEY (1886–1974) was a geologist who was educated at Bristol University and served on Shackleton's Nimrod expedition, working with Professor Edgeworth David before replacing New Zealand geologist Allan Thomson on the *Terra Nova*. After his return, he was awarded an MC for his signal work during the First World War, and his Antarctic research earned him a BA from Cambridge after the war. His highly distinguished career included vice-chancellorships at both Melbourne and Birmingham Universities, the chairmanship of the Royal Commission on the Civil Service (1953–5), and the presidency of the Royal Geographical Society (1961–3). Priestly was knighted in 1949.

CHARLES S. WRIGHT ("Silas;" 1887–1975) was a Canadian physicist on the scientific staff and a member of the first support party; he later participated in the search for Scott's last camp. Wright eventually married one of Raymond Priestley's sisters.

Other Players:

LEON H. B. AMUNDSEN (1870–1934) was Roald Amundsen's older brother and business manager before they had a falling-out over property matters in 1923, ending their relationship.

CLEMENTS R. MARKHAM (1880–1916) was an officer in the Royal Navy in his early years who later served as president of the Royal Geographical Society from 1893 until 1905. As president, Markham oversaw the organization of the National Antarctic

(Discovery) Expedition, which was his crowning achievement. He was also a strong patron of Scott's second or British Antarctic (Terra Nova) Expedition and a habitual denigrator of Shackleton's achievements. As president of the Royal Geographical Society, Markham orchestrated the prevailing allegiance to the deadly strategy of man-hauling. He died when he accidently dropped a burning candle in his own bed.

FRIDTJOF NANSEN (1861–1930) achieved international fame in 1888 by leading the first recorded crossing of Greenland. The great Norwegian explorer, statesman, and humanitarian was Amundsen's mentor and sometimes benefactor.

KATHLEEN BRUCE SCOTT (1878–1947) was the wife of Robert Scott. As the owner of her deceased husband's diaries, she shamelessly edited Scott's criticisms of his subordinates. Kathleen Scott went on to have a successful career as a sculptor, remarrying and eventually assuming, as her second husband's consort, the title of Lady Kennet.

ERNEST H. SHACKLETON (1874–1922) accompanied Scott as third mate on the southern journey during the Discovery Expedition but was sent home early for health reasons. Shackleton considered this a slight by Scott and never forgave him. In 1907, he again set out for the South Pole as commander of the Nimrod Expedition, but was forced, due to foul weather, to turn back just ninety-seven miles from the pole. After the famous Endurance Expedition of 1914–1916, he went south once more, this time on the *Quest*, and died in 1922 while anchored off the coast of South Georgia.

Today, a full one hundred years after Scott's "Message to the Public" gave birth to a legend, Shackleton has soared to eleventh place in the rankings of the "British 100," while Scott has plunged to fifty-fourth place, almost reversing their standings.

TIMELINE OF EVENTS IN AMUNDSEN'S AND SCOTT'S LIFETIMES

While timelines serve as a helpful reference for the sequential ordering of events, the rich warp and weft of human history is far from linear; lives and moments are woven together creating patterns that only emerge when seen from a distance in time. Well before either Scott or Amundsen drew a first breath, the stage was being set for these two remarkable explorers to take their places in the Heroic Age of Polar Exploration.[1]

In 1845, more than a hundred British sailors, led by John Franklin, died of starvation, hypothermia, scurvy, lead poisoning, and cannibalism while attempting an expedition to the Northwest Passage, an event that not only foreshadowed the similar fate of another Royal Navy officer, Robert Scott, but also later captivated young Roald Amundsen's imagination and interest in polar exploration.

Sixty years after Franklin's unsuccessful quest, Amundsen's boyhood dream became a reality when, with the remarkably small crew of only six men sailing the tiny *Gjoa*, he became the first to navigate the Northwest Passage, a tortuous passage threading through the islands, shoals, and ice of Canada's arctic archipelago to the Beaufort and then the Bering Seas. Beginning with Giovanni Verrazano 382 years before, numerous attempts at navigating the passage were made by mostly English explorers, not to explore and settle Canada, but to open up an easy trade route to the wonder of Asian riches. Following this historic feat, Amundsen, who is considered the greatest explorer of all time, simply and humbly wrote in his diary on August 26, 1905:

> My boyhood dream—at that moment it was accomplished. A strange feeling welled up in my throat. I was somewhat overstrained and worn—it was a weakness in me—but I felt tears in my eyes.

Timeline:

1841—James Clark Ross sighted the Great Ice Barrier on his Antarctic expedition.

1847—John Franklin died on June 11 during his search for the Northwest Passage.

1868—Robert Falcon Scott was born to John and Hannah Scott on June 6 in the countryside of Devonport, England.

1872—Roald Engebreth Gravning Amundsen was born in Borge, Sweden (now Norway) on July 16.

1893—Amundsen failed his medical school exams at Christiana and dropped out of school altogether.

1893—Fridtjof Nansen embarked on the *Fram* headed for the North Pole. Nansen and Hjalmar Johansen set a record for distance farthest north, 272 miles from the North Pole.

1894—Amundsen led expert skier Laurentius Urdahl on an unsuccessful ski expedition west of Oslo at Hardangervidda, the largest mountain plateau in northern Europe, with conditions similar to Antarctica, to gain experience skiing on mountainous terrain in the coldest climes.

1894—Amundsen embarked on a sealing expedition to the Arctic

Ocean on the *Magdalena* to learn techniques for sailing in icy waters.

1895—Amundsen received his mate's certification in Norway in May, but with a disappointing second-class rating.

1896—Amundsen and his twenty-five-year-old brother, Leon, made a second attempt on the one-hundred-mile-wide storm-whipped Hardangervidda Plateau in Norway.

1897—At the age of twenty-five, Amundsen embarked on a scientific expedition to Antarctica as second officer on the *Belgica* with American explorer, Dr. Frederick A. Cook, M.D.[2]

1899—Scott met Clements Markham and applied to lead the Antarctic expedition.

1900—Amundsen completed his sea training and gained his master's certification in April.

1901—Scott, as commander of the sailing ship *Discovery*, embarked on his first Antarctic expedition, along with Ernest Shackleton, his third officer, and Dr. Edward Wilson.

1903—Sailing the *Gjoa*, Amundsen embarked on his successful expedition to become the first to navigate the Northwest Passage.

1903—Orville and Wilbur Wright achieved the first sustained airplane flight on December 7 in Kitty Hawk, North Carolina, an event marking the beginning of aeronautic supremacy by the United States, continuing through Lindbergh, Yeager, the Apollo moon landing and more recently, drone superiority.

1904—Scott returned from the Antarctic, becoming a national hero for establishing a new record for Farthest South at 82°17' on December 30, 1902. Scott was promoted to captain on October 11, 1904.[3]

1905—Amundsen completed his navigation of the Northwest Passage, putting him in the pantheon of great explorers, even before being the first to the South Pole. During this expedition, Amundsen also refined the position of the ever-moving North Magnetic Pole.

1908—Scott married Edith Agnes Kathleen Bruce on September 2.

1909—On the Nimrod Expedition, Antarctic explorer Ernest Shackleton came within ninety-seven miles of the South Pole at 88° 23′ S on January 9.

1909—Rear Admiral Robert Edwin Peary, an American Arctic explorer, made the dubious claim to have discovered the North Pole on April 6. He also took soundings proving that the sea around the North Pole is not a shallow body of water, as scientists had previously believed. Another American explorer, Dr. Frederick Cook, M.D., also made the claim to have discovered the North Pole.

1910—On July 16, Scott embarked from England on his second and final trip to Antarctica, commanding the sailing ship *Terra Nova*. A leaker, *Terra Nova* was powered by a steam engine requiring a substantial amount of coal.

1910—On August 9, Amundsen embarked from Norway on his expedition to Antarctica, commanding the *Fram*. Amundsen retrofitted the *Fram* with a diesel engine, a technological advancement that gave instant power in the ice pack precisely when needed.

February 17, 1911—During the depot-laying journey before the spring march to the South Pole, Scott gave the order to turn back at 79° 28 ½′.

April 22—August 24, 1911—The absent sun left both the Norwegians at Framheim and the Brits at Cape Evans in darkness.

October 19, 1911—Amundsen and his crew departed their home base at the Bay of Whales on the Great Ice Barrier headed for the South Pole.

November 1, 1911—Scott and his crew departed their base at Cape Evans on the McMurdo Sound headed for the South Pole.

December 14, 1911—Amundsen and his crew became the first to reach the South Pole.[4]

January 3, 1912—Scott made the impromptu decision for five men, rather than four, to complete the last leg of the journey to the South Pole. Edward "Teddy" Evans, Lashly, and Crean were ordered to return to Cape Evans; they miraculously reached home safely.

January 17, 1912—Five weeks after Amundsen's arrival, Robert Falcon Scott, Henry Robertson Bowers, Lawrence Edward Oates, Dr. Edward Wilson, and Edgar Evans finally reached the South Pole.

January 25, 1912—Amundsen and his crew safely reached their home base, Framheim.

February 17, 1912—Edgar Evans died. Gangrene caused by an infection from an earlier cut on his hand and extreme emaciation aggravated by ostracism by all four officers were the causes of death.

February 24, 1912—At South Barrier Depot, Scott made a diary entry of a significant shortage of paraffin fuel oil. The shortage of fuel caused by the paraffin being stored in improperly sealed cans was repeated at the next depot on March 1.

March 16 or 17, 1912—On or near his thirty-second birthday, suffering from frost-bitten and gangrenous feet, Captain Oates nobly sacrificed his life to keep from slowing down his fellow explorers.

March 21, 1912—Starving and thirsty, Scott, Wilson, and Bowers lay in their sleeping bags ensconced in their tent as their lives ebbed away. Scott made his final diary entry right before he died on March 29, 1912.

August 15, 1914—Britain declared war on Germany, beginning the grueling four-year conflict that lasted until the Armistice on November 11, 1918, ended the First World War.

1915—*Fleet Memorial*, a statue of Robert Falcon Scott executed by his widow, Kathleen Scott, was unveiled. The bronze statue, showing Scott in full polar gear on a granite pedestal, stands at Waterloo Place in London.

1917—A second statue of Scott by Kathleen was unveiled in Christchurch, New Zealand.

1918—Following the plan of Nansen's 1893 attempt, Amundsen began an Arctic expedition, hoping to use ocean currents, proven useful by Nansen, to float over the North Pole on his ship, *Maud*.

1923—John Murray published a one-volume affordable edition of Scott's last journals on September 6; he further expanded Scott's legacy by publishing a "school reader" of excerpts from Scott's last journals.

1924—George Mallory died during his attempted ascent of Mount Everest.

1924—Ponting released a feature-length version of his film about Scott, *The Great White Silence*.

1925—Unable to float the *Maud* over the North Pole because of becoming lodged in pack ice, Amundsen later joined Lincoln Ellsworth, son of a Wall Street multimillionaire, in an unsuccessful attempt to be the first to fly over the North Pole.

1926—With Lincoln Ellsworth and Umberto Nobile, Amundsen flew the dirigible *Norge* over the North Pole. Earlier that year, Americans Richard Byrd and Floyd Bennett claimed to have flown a Fokker airplane over the North Pole.

1927—Charles Lindbergh completed his solo nonstop flight in *The Spirit of St. Louis* from New York to Paris.

1928—Amundsen crashed in the Arctic Ocean while leading a search party for Umberto Nobile on June 18.

1928—Hungarian biochemist Albert Szent-Gyorgyi discovered the use of vitamin C for the prevention of scurvy.

Notes

1. The Heroic Age of Antarctic Exploration defines an era that extended from the end of the nineteenth century to the early 1920s. During this twenty-five-year period the Antarctic continent became the focus of international efforts that resulted in intensive scientific and geographical exploration. Sixteen major Antarctic expeditions were launched from eight different countries during this time. The common factor in these expeditions was the limited resources available to them before advances in transportation and communication technologies revolutionized the work of exploration. This meant that each expedition became a feat of endurance that tested its personnel to physical and mental limits, and sometimes beyond. The "heroic" label, bestowed later, recognized the adversities that had to be overcome by these pioneers, some of whom did not survive the experience; during this period, seventeen expedition members died.
2. Dr. Frederick A. Cook, M.D., demonstrated on this expedition that partially cooked seal meat prevents scurvy, a disease caused by lack of vitamin C.

3. Third Officer Shackleton was not invited to share this distinction of the Farthest South, a slight that was never forgotten and gave rise to an intense, lifelong rivalry with Scott.

4. Duke University Professor Ross D. E. MacPhee, author of Race to the End, points out that December 13, 1911, was the date of discovery. The Norwegians did not account for crossing the international dateline.

APPENDIX: LIST OF FIRSTS BY AMUNDSEN

- First to ski on the Antarctic continent.
- First to sledge on the Antarctic continent.
- First to overwinter on the Antarctic continent.[1]
- First to navigate the Northwest Passage.
- First to establish that the north magnetic pole moves many miles in a few years. (We now know that both the north and south magnetic poles may shift as much as five miles in a year. Both poles are the point where the earth's lines of longitude meet, which can be fifteen hundred miles from the point on the magnetic compass.)
- First to stand on the bottom of the world at −90°, the South Pole
- First to reach point Farthest North. (Lieutenant Commander Robert E. Byrd of the U.S. Navy later claimed to be the first to fly over the North Pole on May 8, 1926.)[2]
- First civilian to get a pilot's license in Norway.
- First to cross the North Pole in a dirigible.
- First ever to reach both −90° and +90°.

- One of the first to elevate the leadership discipline of strategy to an art form.
- One of many to sputter and utterly fail in retirement.

Notes

1. Some of the polar literature uses "winter over" to incorrectly describe staying in Antarctica through June to August. Only northerners heading to Florida winter over!
2. The *Josephine Ford* returned about fifteen-and-a-half hours after takeoff to Kings Bay (now Ny-Alesund), Norway, where Amundsen organized "nine good Norwegian cheers." However, given the known speed of the Fokker airplane that Byrd and Bennett were flying, it has since been established that reaching the North Pole was impossible in that short time frame. In the noble effort of reaching true geographical North, Americans Byrd, Peary, and Cook's moral compass was obviously broken.

CLIFF NOTES ON THE HISTORY OF LEADERSHIP

With tens of thousands of books in print on the subject of leadership and the importance of leadership in nation building, an overview of the history of leadership at the Hubble telescope level is ventured to give context to the teachings of the polar diaries. Since the time of Plato, mankind has studied leadership.

- In the eighteenth century, enlightened philosophers such as Voltaire laid claim that through the application of reason, man could control his destiny.

- In the nineteenth century, a more optimistic belief in progress and the perfectibility of man produced an even rosier world.

- At the end of the nineteenth century, Sigmund Freud and Max Weber destroyed western man's faith and belief in rationality. Freud posited that the unconscious was responsible for much of human behavior. Weber and his followers believed that bureaucracies, even though highly efficient, dehumanize people because of "technical rationality," which is rationality without morality. This was the primary defense pleaded by German Field Marshalls at Nuremburg: I was just a good bureaucrat doing what I was told—just following orders.

Weber believed charismatic leadership was the only means to resist bureaucratization.

- The last fifty years have produced four meaningful leadership theories:

    1. Style theory, which singles out the one style of leadership—one example would be the style captured by the spirit of FDR's America: open, democratic and meritocratic;

    2. Contingency theory, which states that leadership is dependent on the particular situation (Dr. Lane Anderson);

    3. Context theory, which looks at leadership that is primarily anti-bureaucratic and charismatic using four essential leadership qualities:

        - Tough empathy (Amundsen)
        - Leader differences (Condoleezza Rice as a concert pianist)
        - The need for leaders to expose some flaws (Cisco CEO Chambers's dyslexia). The flaw must be collateral to the generalship; bank CEOs best not share with followers an inability to read a cash flow statement.
        - The knowledge of which skills to use in various circumstances. (Former General Hugh Shelton, sixteenth chairman of the Joint Chiefs of Staff)

    4. Trait theory, which attempts to identify the common characteristics of effective leaders.

In the race to the pole, we have two leaders hailing from two nations, with dichotomous leadership styles and polar opposite value systems. Inasmuch as the two polar opposites were leaders in identical circumstances, the leaders' diaries, cross-referenced with the diaries of their followers, provide direct evidence for the readership jury to conclude the following:

- Compassionate entrepreneurial leadership is essential.
- There is no room for egotism in leadership. True humility is its own form of self-confidence.
- While education can help in developing the integrative capacity and catalytic coping necessary for strategy, the diaries provide evidence that superior educational ability is not essential for good leadership. However, even though education is not a leadership trait, it is far better for the leader to have a liberal arts education than no education.
- Common sense is all too uncommon in modern leadership, taking a backseat to intellectualism. Meanwhile, the attending corollary to common sense — good judgment — is not to be confused with being judgmental. Nothing could be further from the truth.
- Charisma is greatly overrated using the evidence from the ice. (Max Weber was wrong; Scott was dead wrong.)
- Great leaders think strategically. (Since situations change quickly, strategic thinking cannot be effectively delegated.)
- Command and control is only effective on the bridge of a warship engaged in battle when split-second following orders decide whether bones are wet or dry.
- Ten leadership traits are present in the diaries (CHALLENGES).
- The leader does not need all ten leadership traits. (Several are sufficient, especially if they are consistency, humility, and authenticity, as practiced by Amundsen.)

Stated in simplest terms, Amundsen packed down his ego and created a workplace for the human spirit. Not only were there ten hands planting the Norwegian flag at −90°, five heads and five hearts were engaged as one singularly determined team. Leadership at its finest.

LEADERSHIP MYTHS

MYTH #1: ANYONE CAN BE A LEADER.

Many wannabe leaders do not have the authentic self-knowledge essential for leadership. Without the requisite discipline to reflect deeply on the valuable leadership lessons of life and learn from this daily self-examination, most fail to become compassionate entrepreneurial leaders.

Another avenue of growth comes with the serious reading of biographies of great men and women, not to emulate, but to understand the context of leadership traits in complex contingency situations. Because authenticity is so important, attempting to copy a particular successful leader is an exercise in futility—there is no substitute for on-the-job training. However, supplementing the many experiences etched on the little cat feet of daily life by reading good biographies about great leaders strengthens your arsenal; the inspirational rhapsody of the biography itself is a bonus.

The kind of dedication required for constant reflection and the pursuit of renewed understanding and knowledge brings us to an important point: individuals must genuinely *want* to be leaders. Many have no interest in hoisting the weight of that responsibility. Moreover, others choose to devote more time to their private lives, avocations, or children: There is a lot more to life than work; there is much more to work than being a boss.

MYTH #2: ALL CEOS, GENERALS, MANAGING DIRECTORS, POPES, AND PRINCIPALS, ARE LEADERS

It is simply not true that all people in leadership positions are leaders. Some achieve numero uno by political acumen, some by accident, some by crisis, and some by deaths of others. If you look at almost any organization, you will find real leaders all over, down the organizational chart even to the shop floor. Title is certainly not a prerequisite for leadership.

The simplest definition of a leader is a person who has followers. In most cases, rank doesn't have much to do with that. The great organizations of tomorrow now realize the urgency of developing leaders down into the ranks.

MYTH #3: BUSINESS RESULTS ALWAYS IDENTIFY A LEADER

If only this were true, picking leaders would be a piece of cake. If it were only this simple, every company in America would have already identified its CEO in the succession plan demanded by all high-performing boards.

Businesses in quasi-monopolistic industries can often do well with competent management rather than great leaders. Win/loss records in sports or quarterly earnings statements (even in the same competitive arenas) are not necessarily indicators of effective leadership. The tyranny of the short term is the real issue and the bane of capitalism. Many well-led enterprises do not necessarily produce results in the short term. The premise that strategy is critical to leadership is defined by long-term results; accordingly, it can be postulated that true leaders deliver results over the long term.

MYTH #4: LEADERS ARE GREAT COACHES

Many suggest that good leaders are and ought to be good coaches for their followers. This does not wash in the real world. Certainly Amundsen and Scott demonstrated no coaching aptitude. To the contrary, Amundsen encouraged his crew to coach *him* on their varying expertise in navigation, skiing, dog handling, and dog training. It is wishful thinking that a person like Amundsen, whose distinctive strength lay in his ability to convince others to march to the end of the Earth, would automatically be able to coach effectively and impart technical skills.

WHY WOULD THESE MEN WILLINGLY SUBJECT THEMSELVES TO SUCH UNTHINKABLE HAZARDS AND HARDSHIPS AS THE ASSAULT ON THE SOUTH POLE?

Explorers like Columbus, La Salle, and John Franklin had the incentive to discover a navigable waterway to the orient to claim the riches. Mallory's failed attempt and Hillary's successful ascent to the top of Mt. Everest (29,028 feet) had no such rationale. Similarly, Nansen's attempt to reach the North Pole through an expanse of frozen sea had no apparent use to anyone either.

Like Nansen, Amundsen's assault on the South Pole had no known commercial value at the time—only the impetus of national pride. Scott's relied on the scientific rationale to justify his risky jaunt to the ends of the earth; this too rings hollow. Scott clearly intended to gain naval rank, but that is hardly a rationale for a death struggle with the ice, mano a mano.

So what drives a person to take such risks?

George Mallory tells us he didn't know the answer with his explanation: "Because it's there." Not just beekeepers like Edmund Hillary are averse to leading examined lives; his elusive explanation is summed up in one quick stab: "If you have to ask, you wouldn't understand." That mankind is hardwired for adventure is another common but totally implausible explanation.

Like the entrepreneurial engineer/inventor who is willing to risk his job, his security, his company, and his reputation over the next big thing, maybe the thrilling rush of adrenalin that comes with the pursuit is the only viable explanation. It is true; if you don't know the overpowering rush that comes with taking on the risky challenge, you really would not understand.

ACKNOWLEDGEMENTS

DR. LANE ANDERSON

Dr. Lane Anderson was an invaluable collaborator on this book due to his uniquely varied careers as a captain in the United States Navy (surface warfare officer, naval intelligence), as a thirty-three-year educator and principal of three schools (designated a National Distinguished Principal), along with being a writer, columnist, and published author. Dr. Anderson continues his twenty-one-year career as a marriage and family therapist in private practice, over fifteen years as a consultant for "high-risk" schools, and an instructor in the Business and Industry Program at Alamance Community College in North Carolina.

In general, there are only two types of friendship: old friendship and new. Old friendships tend to be unconditional. Lane and I bonded into a unique friendship some seven years ago: a new friendship with the unconditional nature of genuine old friendship. We first met at RainMakers, a group of leaders who give pro bono business guidance to entry-level, economically challenged people of all backgrounds as they start a small business. We immediately bonded as though we had known each other our entire lives.

The bedrock of our friendship was our identical experiences

attending Myers Park High School in Charlotte, NC—the school featured in *Life Magazine* in the early 1960s as a new high school model using a college layout of a separate building for each discipline.

Aside from our high school alma mater, our overarching bond was sharing the "Age of Innocence," with its twenty-five-cent gas and the advent of convertibles (with no seat belts, no air bags, and sometimes no brakes), along with a love for beach music, with all of us on the dance floor drinking from the same soda bottle—amazingly, no deaths reported! During those days, there were no parachute parents checking in every second of the day, and, believe it or not, we managed without them.

We lived during that wonderful sliver of time when the world was fully at peace. Drugs, booze, and premarital sex were not part of this era, especially if you were into sports. We were both student-athletes before the term was coined, but "Night Train" Lane was the real deal. Lane and I shared a mutual love of our track coach, Stuart Allen, who was inducted into the NC Hall of Fame in 2005. This was an era of discipline in the home and in school; the idea of a parent bailing us out if we got in trouble was out of the question. They would have no doubt sided with the school authorities! This generation has arguably produced the best risk-takers, problem solvers, thinkers, and innovators in history.

Lane's incredible résumé is relevant to the theme of this book, especially due to his expertise in "situational" leadership, the subject of his doctoral dissertation, which is still used as reference material at the Naval Academy and U.S. War College. In our shared opinion, parenting requires expert leadership, as his best-selling book attests.[1] Additionally, he continues to teach leadership within the context of making organizations more successful, as well as helping to improve the quality of relationships among individuals, couples, and families, the foundation of America's future.

Captain Lane S. Anderson

Notes

1. For more information on Dr. Anderson and his book, Care Enough to Discipline (Third Edition), go to his website: www.CareEnoughToDiscipline.com.

SELECTED BIBLIOGRAPHY

Wherever possible, I went back to the original diaries. Of the many books on polar exploration I read with pleasure, I am listing the books that became reference books in my research.

Amundsen, Roald, *My Life as an Explorer*. Garden City, New York: Doubleday, Doran & Co., 1928.

—, *The North-West Passage*. New York: Dutton, 1908.

—, *The South Pole*. Translated by A. G. Chater. New York: L. Keedick, 1913.

Bown, Stephen R., *The Life of Roald Amundsen*. Boston: Da Capo Press, 2012.

Cherry-Garrard, Apsley, *The Worst Journey in the World*. London: Chatto and Windus, 1965.

Hanssen, Helmer, *Voyages of a Modern Viking*. London: G. Routledge & Sons, 1936.

Huntford, Roland, *The Last Place on Earth*. New York: The Modern Library, 1999.

MacPhee, R.D.E., *Race to the End: Amundsen, Scott and the Attainment of the South Pole*. New York: Sterling Innovation, 2010.

Scott, Captain Robert F., *The Diaries of Captain Robert Scott*, Facsimile Edition. Tylers Green, Buckinghamshire: University Microfilms Ltd., 1968.

—, *The Voyage of the "Discovery."* London: Macmillan and Co., 1905.

—, *Scott's Last Expedition.* London: Macmillan and Co., 1913

Shackleton, E. H., *The Heart of the Antarctic.* London, William Heinemann, 1909.

Sipiera, Paul P., *The World's Great Explorers Roald Amundsen and Robert Scott.* Chicago: The Childrens Press 1990

Smith, Michael, *An Unsung Hero: Tom Crean—Antarctic Survivor.* West Link Park, Ireland: The Collins Press, 2009.

Solomon, S. *The Coldest March: Scott's Fatal Antarctic Expedition.* New Haven, CT: Yale, 2001

Wilson, Edward, *Diary of the "Discovery" Expedition.* New York: Humanities Press, 1967.

—, Diary of the "Terra Nova" Expedition. London: Blandford Press, 1972

ABOUT THE AUTHOR

The only way to truly fathom the depths of trench warfare is through the writings of Corporal Erich Remarque, who fought bayonet to bayonet on the Western Front. Likewise, the best vantage point for learning leadership is through the eyes of a battle-tested, lifelong CEO.

Phil Johnston, J.D., has been the CEO of two public companies in addition to several private microelectronic and biotechnology companies. He has also served on the board of directors of five public companies, including seventeen years on a NYSE-listed board. You are invited to lean in closely as you view the leadership of two world class risk takers, Roald Amundsen and Robert Scott, through the keenly focused lenses of Phil's well-worn horn-rimmed spectacles.

Phil Johnston is the author of four books, including *Success in Small Business is a Laughing Matter*, which a lead article in *Esquire* magazine called "the best book ever written about small business."

Utilizing Amundsen's proven strategies of Blinding Speed and Pace, he graduated forty-eighth in his class from Duke University in only three years with a degree in economics, carefully pacing his studies between bridge games and lacrosse, where he napped during his long stretches on the bench. After his launch into the real world, Phil passed the North Carolina Bar on first sitting, attended NYU business school and enlisted in the infantry, all in preparation for manning the helm in the business world. He served as trustee of the University of North Carolina School of Law for two decades, was named Entrepreneur of the Year by CED, served as Founding Chairman of NCTA, the largest trade association in North Carolina, and has recently been named an Entrepreneurial Fellow at Wake Forest University.